Praise for Navigating The Shift: Th

"Draws together ancient philosophies and modern day science to bring today's changes into clear perspective. A born teacher with a creative mind and unique talent for revealing big patterns as well as small details, Smith lays out the basics on how we can catch the wave of energy coming toward us, and offers advanced techniques for mastering the ride. He generously uses examples from his own journey to connect with readers, and brings abstract concepts down to practical terms. This is a book for serious seekers."
- Max Highstein, M.A., Author of *Intuition Retreat*
www.MaxHighstein.com

~~~~

"In a beautifully insightful and eloquent way, Dr. Michael Smith presents a wonderful blend of personal stories, cases, and profound wisdom throughout the book, with his own unique methods of balancing heart with mind to activate one's own personal 'compass'. A great read for those who want to grasp and gain a deeper understanding about their role and thrive in this uncertain, yet amazing time in Earth's history."
- Argus El'iam, Transformational Visionary Artist
www.ArgusEliam.com

~~~~

"Michael Smith masterfully blends story, humor, personal experiences, and universal spiritual principles to help us make sense of this unprecedented time of change. Practical exercises give readers tools for navigating the choppy waters of our "ascension" process into higher consciousness. This book inspires us, gives us hope, and leaves no doubt that our destiny is to live in a state of balance, fulfillment, and grace."
- Jayn Stewart, writer, healer, spiritual counselor

Also by Michael R. Smith

The Complete Empath Toolkit

Awakening the Genesis Within (with LD Porter)

Navigating The Shift:
Thriving In Earth's New Age

Michael R. Smith, Ph.D.

An Empath Connection Publication

Cover design by Raul Chico Goler
Edited by Jayn Stewart

ISBN-13: 978-1492339519
ISBN-10: 1492339512

Manufactured in the United States of America

For more information, please visit

www.EmpathConnection.com

Acknowledgments

To all of my spiritual teachers, who have come in many forms—human and non-human alike. To my parents, who have shown relentless determination in overcoming obstacles, and who made huge sacrifices to raise their children. To my grandparents, Genereau and Smith, for sharing stories, laughter, and memories, and allowing me the privilege to be part of their DNA lines. To editor Jayn Stewart, for polishing the book and making it shine. To Chico Goler, for creating cover art that is beyond what I could have ever envisioned. To all my wonderful clients, some of whose stories grace these pages, thank you for the privilege of working with you.

And, as always, to the ancestors who speak to us every day, and to our spirit guides, who are working harder for us than any of us, with our limited human perception, can possibly understand.

Table of Contents

"Here is the test to find out whether your mission on earth is complete: If you're alive, it isn't."

- Richard Bach

INTRODUCTION

The topic of ascension and the 'Shift' has fired a collective shot—heard around the world—into the consciousness of humanity. And just like humanity's evolution, this shot is traveling in a zig-zag manner, not a straight line! 'The Shift' conjures up a potpourri of ideas and beliefs ranging from the Apocalypse, telepathy, UFO's, and secret government conspiracies, to the anti-Christ and the return of Jesus.

In these times of rapid societal transformation and change, how can we tell what's "real" and what's hype? We are being invited to surrender to the three hardest words for our egos to accept: *We don't know.* Whether or not communications will be disrupted, solar flares will bring about societal chaos, or earthquakes will wreak havoc is for Creator to handle. One undeniable aspect of the Shift has been happening to all of us for years. Our global consciousness is coalescing around two important questions: *Who are we? Why are we here?* Whether we're fundamentalist Christian or New Age believers, each of us has a panel to sew into the quilt that comprises 'The Shift.' A pastiche of colors, it includes many philosophies and worldviews, and is rich because of its diversity of perspectives. Like a good wine, we experience the subtle flavors that enhance the holistic experience.

A fundamental theme that runs through all of the discussion about the Shift is the following: *We are souls who incarnated in a very important time in history to clean up the messes of the past and make better decisions this time around, individually, and collectively, so that we can make the leap into a higher realm of consciousness.*

This book is not a guide about any particular theology, belief, or cosmology. For example, it's not about the Bible or Christianity's version of the apocalypse, nor the Mayan version of what happens beyond 2012. It's not about the end of the world. Or maybe it is. It might be more accurate to say it is about the *end of the world as we have known it.* This book is about hope, inspiration, and placing transformational changes in a broad, hopeful context. This collection of stories, thoughts, and personal exercises will cut through the confusion and expose you to your larger mission. Why exactly are you on the planet at such a transformational time in history? The central theme of this book is that we are all contributing, each in our own way, to assisting with what is called the Shift, or The Ascension. It is my hope that you will be inspired into action toward your Highest Self, truly reaching for the stars, literally! We each have an important role to play in moving toward the Light.

Let's get to it!

Chapter 1

What's All the Fuss?

There is a phenomenal amount of theory, opinion, and research about these exceptional times in which we live. In this chapter, it is not my intention to explore with any depth the academic theories on the new era on Earth, but rather, expand upon and synthesize of some of the significant ideas in the fields of anthropology, mythology, and theology. A partial list of the significant authors includes John Major Jenkins, Gregg Braden, Dr. Anthony Aveni, Lawrence Joseph, Robert Bauval, Graham Hancock, Dr. Alberto Villoldo, Dr. Jose Arguelles, Geoff Stray, and David Wilcock. These writers have made important contributions to our understanding of humanity.

Dr. Jose Arguelles published one of the first books that captured mainstream attention on the topic of a spiritual shift. That book was *The Mayan Factor: Path Beyond Technology,* and more than any other book, it catapulted the important year of 2012 and the concept of a spiritual shift into our collective consciousness. Other important works followed, including *Maya Cosmogensis 2012* by John Major Jenkins and Gregg Braden's *Fractal Time: The Secret of 2012 and a New World Age*, both of which explored the contributions of the Mayan culture in the evolution of consciousness.

The Mayan Calendar

Thousands of years ago, a mysterious culture suddenly appeared, as if out of nowhere, in very inhospitable areas of Mexico's Yucatan Peninsula. Over a relatively short period of time, the culture expanded into what is now Guatemala, Belize, and Honduras. They stayed around for a thousand years. Then, just as mysteriously as it appeared, the culture essentially vanished. Although scientists, archeaologists, and other experts have no definitive conclusions about what exactly happened, there is little doubt that much of our awareness about the important historical time in which we live originates with the Mayan culture's precise, advanced system of recording time.

The Mayan calendar is made up of a series of measurements within measurements, so to speak, and includes several repeating cycles of time. To the Maya, time was not linear, but cyclical. Their perception of time was influenced by their profound fascination with and astute observations of the stars.

The so-called 'long count' calendar is thought to have originated at one Mayan site, Izapa, in southern Mexico, and is called "The Great Cycle." This calendar is filled with juicy hieroglyphic illustrations that show how connected the Mayans were to the heavens. In one particularly interesting set of stone monuments, they showed their own version of the creation. In it, the authors depict that the human ego must fall before the Divine Self can be reborn.

The Mayan calendar 'ended' on December 21, 2012, when a rare galactic alignment between the sun, the Earth, and the center of the Milky Way Galaxy occurred. This alignment happens once every 26,000 years.

Reflecting on this auspicious fact, Jenkins distilled the meaning of the Mayan calendar into one brilliant passage which he believes is the authentic prophecy regarding our new age: "Self-serving egoism will be ruling and running the world, tricking people into forgetting their eternal natures and identifying with their most limited selves. The second part of the prophecy is that ego can humble itself, surrender its illusory belief that it is the true center, and reconnect with the eternal divine self."

Jenkins came to this conclusion through deciphering the messages in pictorial form through glyphs on the monuments in Izapa. Not surprisingly, according to Jenkins, hallucinogenic plant medicines used in rituals and ceremonies have been found, which suggest that these plants were used by the Mayans in a shamanic manner to achieve some of their advanced visions. And thankfully, the ritual use of plant medicines for therapeutic and even psychiatric purposes is becoming less stigmatized in our new era, which may allow us to achieve similar powerful knowledge. Recently, an international scientific symposium was held on the use of medicinal plants in psychiatry. It gained mainstream coverage on CNN, Huffington Post, and all the major news sites. This is good news because it shows that our cultural conditioning to view psychoactive substances as dangerous is lessening. There can be profound medicine contained in the proper ceremonial use of certain plants when done with experienced shamans or keepers of wisdom. "There are a number of trials underway throughout the world....using psychedelic drugs," says Dr. Benjamin St. John Sessa in the journal *Progress in Neurology and Psychiatry*. "The future looks bright for the research potential of (these) drugs....as prescription medicines."

What if all the spiritual yearning, learning, reflecting—everything we think are new thoughts brought about by this New Age—were actually encoded on stone carvings from a mysterious civilization thousands of years ago? If so, were they tapping into the future? Or are we tapping into the past? Or both? Just one reason that many indigenous cultures call the Divine the "Great Mystery."

Correlations With Other Systems of Thought

It is important to note that most major theologies and cultures refer to some prophesied time of transformation. Egyptians, Islamic astrology, and cultures all over the world, from Asia to Africa, refer to periods of great catastrophe and dissolution of society. From the Hindu Prophecy (Kali Yuga, the end time of man) to the Aztec prophecy (Time of the Sixth Sun) to the Egyptian Prophecy (the stone calendar at the Great Pyramid), stories referring to times of transformation are deeply embedded in humanity.

For example, the prophecies of the Hopi tribe, who reside in the Four Corners area of Arizona, New Mexico, Utah and Colorado, have had a profound effect on the current worldview surrounding our spiritual era. Hopi chief Frank Waters' excellent *Book of the Hopi* explores these prophecies in detail. The basic message is that the history of humanity consists of Seven Worlds (periods of time). We are currently moving into The Fifth World. This time will coincide with a time of prophesied "great purification." Native American traditions, including the Lakota Sioux and the Seneca, among many others, refer to the times in which we live as vitally important.

For the plains tribes, including the Lakota Sioux, the buffalo has long been a sacred animal. The buffalo willingly offered itself to take care of the people. Its sacrifice allowed communities to thrive; thus, it was a symbol of abundance. Every portion of the animal was used for some purpose, whether for food, clothing, or sacred tools. The skull, for instance, is used in important ceremonies and adorns altars. Over the years, just like the Native American traditional culture, the buffalo were hunted almost to extinction by the white man. And yet, even as the buffalo were disappearing, the elders knew that they would return.

There's a story in some plains tribal circles that goes like this: When the time of the White Buffalo comes, the elders know that the return of the red man will come about and a great healing of the Earth will begin. According to Jamie Sams, a well-known Native American author who has shared many sacred teachings, "After the time when the buffalo returned, the generation following the flower children would see the dawning of the Fifth World of Peace." That happened in 1994 when a White Buffalo calf was born, fulfilling a 2,000-year-old prophecy among the Sioux tribes. Its birth sparked a firestorm of media coverage around the globe.

The return of the White Buffalo was meant to signal a return to spiritual harmony and balance. In the Sioux belief system, the "hoop of life" is being mended. The "medicine circle" is being closed. Any gaps in the circle are being filled by individuals who are making the commitment to help heal humanity and the Earth. And yet, getting back into harmony with nature may include some potentially rough times, with some elders speaking of coming earthquakes and destruction.

Christianity has its own stories about the Apocalypse and the resurrection of Jesus, which many evangelical Christians believe is happening now. Although it provides no specific date, the Book of Revelation in the *Bible* talks about the end times. It refers to the Rapture, the moment right before Armageddon, when true believers will be lifted up to heaven to watch a great spiritual battle unfold on Earth.

Whether you agree with or can even fathom these interpretations, the stories show humanity's deeply embedded search for meaning concerning times of great transformation.

Scientific Evidence of Rapid Change

Magnetic Shifts: Every few million years, the Earth experiences magnetic pole reversals. Gregg Braden presents evidence which suggests that we are in the early stages of this happening again. He states that before a pole reversal two things happen: first, there are abrupt changes in weather patterns, and second, there is a weakening of the planet's magnetic field. Both events are occurring right now, according to Braden.

He presents a model, "magnetic glue," to explain what is happening. Higher magnetic fields hold us in place, metaphorically and literally. Areas of the world with the highest magnetic fields, such as Russia, tend to embrace change slowly. Other areas of the world with the lowest magnetic field readings, such as California and the West Coast, allow people to embrace change more quickly and move into new states of being. (The greatest technological and social innovation in the United States have long come from the West Coast.)

In the "magnetic glue" model, consciousness itself is influenced by the magnetic fields. The Earth has lost 7 percent of her magnetism over the last 100 years, and it doesn't appear to be stopping. So what does this mean for consciousness itself? Braden demonstrates that with less and less magnetism holding our rigid thought patterns and behaviors in place, we are headed into new territories of human experience. Clinical hypnotherapist and researcher Dr. John Jay Harper, in his book *Tranceformers: Shamans of the 21st Century*, adds "This shift of the electromagnetic field of the planet will bring about a new heaven and a new Earth, a 'telepathic society' capable of creative solutions to problems almost spontaneously as they arise; indeed we will be manifesting miracles beyond our wildest imagination. In no uncertain terms, the communication channel we had to God in the Garden of Eden is opening up within us again."

The effect of magnetic fields on our consciousness is something we each experience every month, as the moon's magnetism interacts with the Earth's. Physicians and law enforcement officials know that violence, psychotic episodes, and rates of hospital admissions spike on full moons. Spiritual leaders across the world plan ceremonies in line with new moons and full moons when magnetic energy is at its peak. These magnetic polarities help us shift into new awareness. As we navigate through this New Age, we must honor the cycles of magnetism, as indigenous societies do, with ceremonies and offerings to the sun and moon. These rituals are explored more fully in my book, *The Complete Empath Toolkit.*

Sunspots: Just as Earth's magnetism changes over time, so does the sun's. Cycles of intense magnetic storms, called sunspots, were originally noticed by Galileo. According to a prediction from the National Center for Atmospheric Research, the coming periods of sunspot activity will be some of the most intense ever recorded and will be 30 to 50 percent higher than the last major sunspot period. This may very well lead to disruption of daily life around the globe. The last major sunspot activity was in 1958. At that time, however, lives didn't depend on satellites and advanced communications technology, which are at the mercy of sunspots.

Synthesis of Views

Awhile back, I posted a blog about Mayan elder Carlos Barrios, a historian, anthropologist and investigator. Barrios studied with traditional elders for 25 years and became a Mayan Ajq'ij, a ceremonial priest and spiritual guide. He also interviewed nearly 600 traditional Mayan elders to widen the scope of his knowledge. This information is found in his book, *The Book of Destiny: Unlocking the Secrets of the Mayans and the Prophecy of 2012.*

Barrios says that Mayan Daykeepers have always viewed

December 21, 2012 as a rebirth, the start of the World of the Fifth Sun. "Many powerful souls have reincarnated in this era, with a lot of power. This is true on both sides, the light and the dark. High magic is at work on both sides. Things will change, but it is up to the people how easy it is for the changes to come about."

I include Barrios' remarks because his affirming view is in line with what many of us are thinking and experiencing. "Everyone is needed," says Barrios. "You are not here for no reason. Everyone who is here now has an important purpose. This is a hard, but a special time. We have the opportunity for growth, but we must be ready for this moment in history."

The basic message? Things are "up for grabs." We're moving from one age into another, from one way of thinking into a new paradigm. Our views of reality will be radically altered. Exactly what that world will look like is up to us. We find ourselves asking a series of questions, to which we do not yet know the answers:

What will our social structures look like?
What will our families look like?
How will we gain access to food?
Will there be currency?
Will we have adequate water?

The answers can be found in one simple term: TBA. To Be Announced.

The announcement is humanity's future.

The announcer? God. Or ourselves, for the two are absolutely indistinguishable.

Get ready, for this journey will take your breath away!

Chapter Two

The Big Picture: Seeing With the Eyes of God

One of the first things I was told when I began my shamanic training with Native American elders was that I was embarking on a quest to answer the following question: Who am I?

And that's what this book is about as well. This chapter will help you understand Who You Are, especially as it relates to The Big Picture.

To understand the important age in which we live, we want to understand who we are. And 'who we are' is not necessarily who we think we are. We are big and we are small. We are light and we are dark. The terrain of our total being includes smooth surfaces and rough edges. We navigate choppy waters and calm seas. We are suns, moons, asteroids, and everything in between. In the *Bible* in the gospel of Luke (12:7), a beautiful phrase illustrates this concept: "Every hair on your head is counted." This poetic example soothes us and lets us know that there are no accidents. There is a spiritual Force guiding us that is greater than any of us can understand. Our goal in this new age is to acknowledge the presence of that Force with great sincerity.

Who We Are: The Ego

We acknowledge that part of our human divinity includes a small mind, otherwise known as the human ego. For better or worse, we must learn to accept and even embrace our small mind. This can be a challenge because the small mind can be tyrannical and selfish. The ego believes that it's directing the show. The ego is the place of complete self-interest, and it believes that it is supreme, separate, and superior. It believes that it knows. That is its job. It's neither good nor bad. It just *is*.

I often hear individuals proclaim that they want to "lose the ego," or "get rid of the ego." These are understandable sentiments, and yet, since we are human, that is asking a lot. It is very likely an impossible task while we are in human bodies, because the small mind does prevent us from driving our cars off of cliffs!

What most of us are really asking for is to have a better *balance* between our Highest Selves and our small minds. The human ego does help us see the world in a certain way. It takes the data it receives and makes that data easy to understand. Its job is to limit, compartmentalize, and do everything in its power to give us a feeling of control and mastery. This can be helpful, for without it we would be overwhelmed in a sea of energy and information.

The workings of the ego are a little bit like the workings of a machine in a sausage factory, except that what is being shaped is our daily experiences. Data comes in and the ego chops it up into pieces that appear to make sense. This works, up to a certain point. We are realizing that we cannot rely *only* on our small minds. We are seeing that the belief that we are separate from each other, from the rocks, from the birds, and from everything, is a total and utter fabrication of the ego.

Who We Are: The Shadow

Early in my training, my spiritual mentor had me learn how to work with fire. One day, as 11 of us were huddled around a fire pit eating cheese sandwiches, my mentor instructed me to build a fire. Feeling tentative, I managed to arrange the kindling, stack a few small branches, light the fire and get it going. However, no sooner had the fire started moving vertically than I was overcome with fear that it might go out. At that moment, the fire began a rapid decline. As I frantically rearranged the logs into something resembling a forest decimated by a tornado, the oxygen was sucked away. Within 60 seconds the fire was down to nothing. Not even a single flame. There were barely enough coals to relight it. I fumbled and fumbled, pleading with it to come back, trying in vain to get air flowing.

I heard voices saying that I was stupid and worthless. I didn't know that these voices were not mine. I didn't know that these voices were just the energy of the Shadow trying to prevent me from doing my job, and that I could simply ignore them. I did not know that I could exist in confidence and centeredness while still being aware of the voices of the Shadow. I erroneously believed that because I could perceive these negative thoughts through my own mind, that must mean that they originated from me. I did not realize then that this is a common misconception. In actuality, many of us who are intuitive simply perceive Shadow energy from others, or Shadow energy from our collective 'past.' But it's not us.

My mentor was sitting no more than 2 feet from me and watching my every panicked move. It was at that point that I experienced one of many "hard-to-believe-I-actually-saw-that" moments.

"Here's how it's done," he said. He motioned toward the fire with his head. It was as if he had poured lighter fluid on the fire. It went from zero to 60, completely ablaze in a matter of 2 seconds, all with his mind. I was stunned. I knew his power was strong; I had seen him walk through a raging fire a few other times and not be burnt in the slightest. My mentor rarely revealed the true depth of his powers in public, and this was one of those rare occasions. I was humbled. This gave me confidence that the Shadow could indeed be overcome.

After a few months of amateurish attempts, I started to get the hang of the fire. My confidence rose as I learned that I could talk to it, listen to it, and especially, have a reciprocal relationship with it. When I purposefully sent the fire my gratitude for keeping us warm, it would crackle or the logs would move at that exact moment. I began to realize this was no coincidence; the fire was responding to my thoughts! I started dialoguing with the fire as if it were another person. Most importantly, I gained confidence that I could exist, and even thrive, without being harmed by the voices and energy of the Shadow that I perceived.

The Shadow is a real spirit that would prefer that all of us remain unconscious and unaware. Its purpose is to keep us disconnected from spiritual awareness. But in the new age, we accept the Shadow as a part of God and realize that it can actually be a force to move us to the Light. By testing us, it makes us stronger and requires us to create more Light energy to stave it off.

Before an important ceremony in 2008, my mentor put us through an initiation ritual which most tribal societies have used. In the old days, they used to defecate and urinate on the aspiring leaders of the tribes, and, if the medicine person didn't flinch, he or she passed the test. My mentor led a group of us out into the woods, and then, with a shovel, he began to cover us in horse manure. I had heard stories about this from my older spiritual brothers and sisters, so I was somewhat prepared for it. As the sun was shining through the trees, I chose to focus on the sun and the heat that felt so good against my skin. Before long, I didn't even realize that I was covered in wet manure. This is what is being asked of us in our new age: to acknowledge and accept the Shadow forces, and yet not let them control us. We are being asked to focus on Light instead.

Darkness and Light go hand in hand. We must experience one polarity in order to experience the other. If we didn't have darkness, we could not have Light. "Unbenknowst to itself, the Shadow serves God," is one of the best descriptions I've heard that explains this concept. Indeed. The Shadow is a part of God. And it serves us by making us stronger, by turning us into fierce spiritual warriors whose weapon of choice is the sustained use of Light energy to send the darkness packing. (FYI to the darkness: *Where you're going, you won't need a Uhaul!*).

I write these words to offer you encouragement to persevere over whatever hardships are currently testing you. Every time we make a decision that moves us toward the Light, there are Shadow forces that do not want us to change. Everything wants to grow and develop, including your limitations. It's not as spooky as it may seem; there is nothing out there that can harm us unless we let it. The one sure thing that will stop darkness from moving forward is by creating massive amounts of Light energy. Your job is to keep moving forward despite the obstacles. If you fall down seven times, you get up eight times. Do not quit. Do not let the Shadow win. Thank the Shadow for helping you move forward. Acknowledge it, accept it, and then move forward by holding the vision of the good things that you want to create.

Who We Are: Not Separate

In Lakota, a phrase is said after every prayer. It is similar to the Christian version of "Amen." The simple and elegant words are "Mitakue Oyasin." These words refer to our connection with the community rather than with the individual. The phrase translates to "We are related to everything."

Our modern culture has become detached from this perspective. We have been tricked by advertising into believing multiple illusions about who we are. We view the Earth as separate from us—something to be mastered and controlled. How else can we explain the destruction of rainforests, preserves, and wilderness? Profound denial and dysfunction have been the hallmarks of the last 300 years, ever since the Industrial Revolution which focused on small parts as if they existed independent from a larger reality.

"It's really, really simple," my teacher intoned to me in 2004. The gears of my brain were spinning. What on Earth could be so simple? Aren't there subtle layers of everything? Doesn't noticing those subtle layers require the ability to analyze, synthesize, and discern? I felt him smiling at me with amusement. It is a challenge, if not an impossibility, to express a concept, truth, or perspective to anyone. Each of us must have our own experience for a particular idea to make sense. We can facilitate a subtle awareness for others and promote a loosening of the psychic grip, and that's about it. Most of us must experience something in our own way, through our unique perception of reality, before a concept that is shared through language begins to make sense.

And so it was that during my first important spiritual ceremony, a vision quest, where we ventured out into the wilderness for four days and four nights without food or water, communing with nature and offering a sacrifice as a means of strengthening our prayer. When I look back with the benefit of the perspective of time, I realize that I had no idea why I was doing what I was doing. My heart knew, and my soul knew, but my intellect did not. My mentor knew this and used it for my benefit, with the goal of connecting my heart and mind.

At the pinnacle of anticipation and anxiety, at the precise moment before we were to be put "out on the hill" and begin our ceremonial explorations into spiritual dimensions, my mentor posed one question. I quivered inside and out. The question was, "For what reason do you ask to go on vision quest?" I searched for the right words but was only able to offer a weak answer. I mumbled something about looking into my heart to understand the reason. My spiritual sister, Bella, spoke up loudly and offered the reason why I did these ceremonies. "For the people," she said clearly and firmly.

The reverberations of this moment still echo in my heart. There is rarely a day that goes by when I am not aware that my life has been structured through karma and a decision that my Higher Self made. In silent moments of reflection, some small understanding of that decision will touch the outer edges of my heart and permeate my consciousness.

I don't write for myself, I write for others. I don't pray for myself, I pray for others—because in praying for others, I am actually praying for myself.

Here's an experiment to illustrate this:

1. Create a feeling of love in your heart.
2. Cup your hands together in front of your heart and ask that this feeling of love be present in your hands.
3. After the feeling has become strong, "blow" on this energy, and with your intention ask   that it be sent to someone who needs it.
4. Notice how this makes you feel.

Depending on the strength of the energy you create, you may feel a change in your own energy after you send love to someone else. Ask yourself: How does that happen?

How is it that when you send love to another person, you also perceive a feeling of love coming back, amplified? What's the natural conclusion? If you create feelings of love and immediately get feelings of love back, what does that mean about differences or perceived separation between you and another person?

The only logical conclusion: there is none.

It may take a good portion of our lives to truly understand that there is no separation between you and me. This isn't an intellectual theory. Those of us who are empaths understand this on a physical and emotional level. We can feel other people in our own bodies. It goes well beyond sympathy. Empaths will actually experience another person's emotions, thoughts, or physical experiences, and are often more painfully aware of another person than the person him or herself.

Here's an example: *what are you noticing right now in your heart area?* You may perceive lightness, tension, sadness, or joy. Whatever you experience, the act of bringing thoughtful awareness to your heart area makes that area flow more freely with energy. Always.

This focus on awareness is one of our functions in this new age— to help other people understand when they are operating or vibrating at less than optimal states of existence. Nothing more, nothing less. It's pretty simple, really. And yet the ego demands complexity just for the sake of intellectual stimulation!

Empaths are just one part of the spectrum of human experience. I propose that even if you do not identify with being an empath, you too can feel other people in your body but perhaps you haven't yet realized when this occurs. This is understandable. The lack of a defined boundary between individuals can confuse even the most skilled intuitive empaths.

The radical thought that you are comprised of me and that I am comprised of you might meet with some resistance. I see evidence of in this in the Comments section of some of my YouTube videos. A recent commenter proclaimed, "I ain't buying taking on other people's physical pain, that's lame." This is an example of the stranglehold that the ego has on our perception of reality. Just because you have never experienced a particular phenomenon, does it mean that it, therefore, must not exist? According to the ego, or the small mind, the answer is yes.

It's analogous to taking a photograph of your kitchen. Because you took a picture of your kitchen, does that mean that your bedroom doesn't exist? Of course not! Similarly, imagining "scientifically unexplainable" phenomena to be out of the frame of a camera lens is a way to allow the ego to understand some of the esoteric phenomena we encounter on our journey to higher states of consciousness. If some of the concepts in this book are new to you, give yourself permission to say, *I don't know.* Saying those three little words provides a world of relief from the pressures of attempting to understand.

Ascension Happens!

Something is happening out there in the universe. For most of our lives—some of us more than others—we've lived underneath the warm, comfortable blankets of our egos. Underneath those blankets we felt safe, at ease, and in control. Now those blankets are being removed. For some, they are being removed in one quick motion due to trauma or near-death experiences. Those comfortable covers, which we thought were so helpful, have shielded us from Who We Really Are. And sometimes that awareness can be painful.

When those shields are removed, we are open to a whole array of new experiences. It can be quite a shock to realize we're not alone in the world. It can be terrifying to realize that our thoughts, which we previously thought were private and only affected us, actually affect others. It can be even more frightening to realize that *we are being watched.* Yes, we are being seen, heard, felt, discovered, and uncovered. And it's ourselves—that part of us connected to the Divine—that is doing the watching. The process of discovering our power can feel like walking out naked onto 5th Avenue in New York City!

It is a common experience for many of us who are awakening to feel a bubble of isolation and perceived 'craziness,' not yet realizing that our psychic perception actually is helpful. What if you knew that the modern world was crazy, and you were the sane one? Would this help to lessen some of the burden?

I primarily focus my counseling and coaching practice in working with individuals who have psychic ability and are just coming out of the spiritual closet, so to speak. They say things like, "I feel like I am going crazy," and "You're going to think I am nuts, but...." It can become humorous, actually, because we are so similar to each other, yet the ego wants to keep us so blind! It's gratifying to help clients realize that they are not as isolated as their small minds would have them believe. They do not, and we do not, exist in a vacuum.

With that in mind, here is a partial list of some of the more intense manifestations of the Ascension, as the Earth shifts into a higher vibration:

* Telepathic Communication: hearing words from spirit or from other people.
* Increased clairvoyant, clairsentient, and clairaudient experiences.
* Intense dreaming experiences, including precognitive dreams. Vivid visions that are unexplained. Seeing little blips of light or energy in your peripheral vision.
* A desire to learn about Native American and indigenous cultures and systems of healing.
* Angelic communication.
* After-death communication or sensing the presence of departed loved ones.
* Inability to accept or tolerate deception, in oneself or others.
* Seeing "ghosts" or other unexplained images in your peripheral vision.
* Operating in the astral realm.
* UFO phenomena.
* Strong feelings of Deja Vu.
* Feelings of dizziness, sometimes accompanied by feelings of depersonalization (watching yourself from a detached perspective).
* An interest in your past lives and receiving glimpses of those while in hypnosis or trance.
* Altered relationship with time: feeling that time is moving quicker than ever, or moments of it dissolving completely into feelings of timelessness.
* Wanting to learn about the "medicine" of animal allies.
* Increased instances of synchronicity (things that might be explained as coincidence).

* Fascination with numeric codes; certain number patterns showing up repeatedly.

All of these are messages from the universe. When these phenomena occur, it's as if spirit is holding up a mirror and asking us to see more of ourselves. We may not understand why we see certain configurations, and yet we can take comfort in the fact that when they show up, it is the spiritual realms' way of tapping us on the shoulder. They are letting us know that they are around, that they are listening. They are more a part of our life than we can possibly understand. We are constantly showered with compassion from the spirit world. Our ancestors, guides, and friends are on guard for us, giving us messages of hope, clarity, and understanding. Our only job is to listen a little better!

Noticing and Embracing Your Unique Gifts

If you're reading this book, you have asked (whether you're aware of it or not) to structure your life in a certain way. With full awareness, before birth, you set forth the parameters and framework of your current life. You carry certain energies, talents, gifts, and skill sets—what some indigenous elders would call your unique "medicine."

It is no accident that you are on planet Earth at this moment in history, that you are reading these pages—anxious, eager, and willing to explore the outer edges of who you really are. You are ready to discover that which is at your center. You are the rocket ready for launching, counting down to the moment when you will be able to soar into the heavens and finally, finally, after all these years, see yourself as you really are—to see yourself with the eyes of God.

To give you an idea about who you might be, I will use an example from my own life. I love writing. There is something riveting about the way my fingers caress the keyboard, sailing smoothly over the black keys, crisply depressing the keyboard and forming strange symbols into something that coveys meaning, depth, and, hopefully, inspiration to others. The process of expressing the deepest recesses of my soul in this manner is enthralling.

At times I wonder, what is it about my soul that is able to effortlessly express thoughts in words? At times I have wished to be the rock star on stage, flailing away at the drums, keeping the beat to a really pumped-up song. At other times I have wished to be the mezzo soprano, stirring pure emotion through a captivating voice. At other times still, I have hoped and prayed, with every fiber of my being, that I could be a political leader in my community, forming legislation and policy that helps the people.

In comparison to these other desires, I must confess that at times, being a writer seems mundane. And yet *something* led to the writing of this book despite my occasional desire to have a sexier profession. What *is* that something? Whatever it is, it manifested itself early. As a one-year-old child, my mother said that I would sit "for hours on end" turning the pages of books that I did not know how to read.

Interesting notice.

This mysterious force led me to ask for a typewriter for Christmas at age 7 so I could start a neighborhood newspaper.

Another interesting notice.

This soul-level gravitation led me to become the editor of my high school paper, winning several state writing awards and eventually gaining a scholarship to Saint John's University, where I was a writer on the college paper. It also led me to complete 8 scholarly journal publications and a Ph.D. dissertation by the time I was 30.

Hmmm. Might something be asking for my attention?

I share this story to motivate you to examine your own life story. In the same way that I have "noticed" (we'll explore the importance of that word later) things that come easily to me, I ask you to review your life and observe your interests and talents. Why are you who you are? What is it about your gifts and talents that comes easily for you? Why has your career taken the trajectory it has? Why is it that you are a nurse, helping others in their darkest hours of physical pain? Why is it that you are the personal trainer, tuned in to the physics of motion, movement, sport, and weights? Why is it that you have such an interest in nutrition and diet and want to help others achieve optimum health? Why does being a salesman come easily for you?

What is it about YOU that has led you, seemingly with little effort, to be the one who is a broadcaster, a gymnast, a teacher?

A clue to these mysterious questions may be found in the word *karma.*

In the New Age Karma Is Acknowledged

If we tune the satellite dishes of our awareness to the proper channels, Spirit offers us clues of who we are. We receive glimpses, like a mirror.

One of my earliest memories from childhood is repeatedly dreaming of being on a ship in the ocean and suddenly sinking underwater. My three-year-old brain couldn't make sense of these images, and yet I was deathly afraid of the water. Why did I fear for my mother's life when she traveled on a cruise ship? Why did my throat close up at the mere thought of being on a boat? Why did it constantly throb, so much that I wouldn't wear a shirt unless it had a collar?

Might my Highest Self have been speaking to me? Might I have been tuned in to the energy that I was carrying from another lifetime in which I drowned? Might it have to do with healing that energy?

Karma is a Sanskrit word that has origins in Hindu, Sikh, and Buddhist traditions. It relates to the cause-effect relationship between what we create (or have previously created) and what we experience. The concept has woven its way into the mainstream with common expressions such as, "You reap what you sow," "You get what you give," "Garbage in, garbage out," and "What goes around comes around." We understand, on an intuitive level, that what we think about is what we will experience.

If you want to know who you are, you will find it reassuring that many others are asking the same questions. Past-life therapist and medical doctor, Brian Weiss, author of *Through Time Into Healing*, says that learning about one's past lives offers "a rapid method of treating psychiatric symptoms, symptoms that had previously taken many months of costly therapy to alleviate." He says that learning about our past lives gives us a "much more direct way to heal pain and fear." Learning about our past lives can also help the ego make sense of symptoms that may be remnants from another time. And that, in turn, can motivate us to be energetically clear so that we may experience a more free-flowing life.

In his stunning book, *Vibrational Medicine: The #1 Handbook of Subtle Energy Therapies,* Dr. Richard Gerber talks about the little-known fact that Jesus taught about reincarnation. However, these portions of the *Bible* were deleted by a powerful Catholic pope who felt that this message would threaten his power. Even Jesus' resurrection showed that consciousness can survive bodily death. Dr. Gerber summarizes the point of reincarnation by saying that during each lifetime the incarnating soul partakes of diverse experiences which allow it to experience the wonders, joys, and sorrows of human existence. Eventually, he asserts, each soul will experience "every conceivable variation of human form," and through each of these experiences, the soul comes to know itself. That is precisely what is happening on Earth right now. The veils that have prevented us from perceiving other dimensions of reality, including memories of our past lives, are now coming off.

"Spiritual friction" occurs when our present experiences activate past decisions and painful experiences that have yet to be healed and integrated. We all are carrying experiences like this, some more than others, that are activated when we encounter situations that take us back to lower vibrations created in some other dimension or existence. It is much more than a simple representation of the past. It *is* the past, occurring right now, simultaneously. (For example, when I encounter very strong lower-vibratory energy, the right part of my head will sometimes experience sharp, intense pain. I believe that this spot represents a past wound that is asking for healing).

Spirit gave me a message one day: I heard, "You were Robinson Crusoe in that lifetime." Being the good spiritual detective that I am, I researched that book, the character, and especially the author, Daniel Defoe. Might his life contain clues to energies that are in my own? Was I Daniel Defoe? This is a trick question that may never be fully answered, at least not in this lifetime. It's a question designed to trap the ego into a yes or no answer. A better question might be, 'What is it about Daniel

Defoe's lifetime that I can learn from?' or 'How can I use the knowledge of Daniel Defoe to learn about myself?'

In much the same way as I would ask this question, now is the time to ask yourself questions about parts of your soul that can inform your current existence. If we ask from our hearts, gently and softly, without demanding, God may give us glimpses of answers to the fundamental questions Who Am I? and Why Am I Here? Ask yourself why you are attracted to certain time periods. Why do you remember certain images? Why are you drawn to certain paintings? Why do you feel comfortable in houses with a certain style of furniture? Why do you like the foods you like? What about your clothes? Do they reflect a certain history or culture?

What is it about certain cities or places in the world that you find attractive? Why are you attracted to certain books, authors, movies, or genres of art? Have you ever stopped to consider the implications of your desires? What is it about the things that nurture your soul (as opposed to your lover's or neighbor's) that give reassurance and comfort? Might these attractions, which might be labeled "tastes" or "preferences," reflect some part of your soul that lived at another time?

Exercise: Connecting with our Past Selves

1. Using the ages 5, 10, 15, 20, 25, etc., as benchmarks, examine your achievements and career interests at each point in your life. What were you doing? What projects were you involved in? What activities did you enjoy? At each age, what did you want to be when you grew up?

2. Now take a moment to notice the central theme of each age, in terms of what you were *creating*. Is there a pattern in how your soul chose to express itself? How was your soul attempting to manifest its unique desires in the world?

3. If you notice a theme, ask your Highest Self for inspiration to

complete the following sentence, and use it as an affirmation, "My soul expresses itself through _____ because I came into this life with a unique talent for _____."

4. Repeat the sentence, voicing it aloud several times and using it as an affirmation. The physical act of voicing an affirmation not only helps create more positive energy, the repetition also helps the brain and nervous system accept what you are saying as truth. Ask that you receive guidance and inspiration for continued learning about your unique gifts, especially through your dreams. Then let it go and trust that the answers will show up.

Because I work primarily with empaths and highly sensitive people, it has been my observation that these individuals carry a great deal of karma in their physical, emotional, and spiritual bodies. They carry it especially for their immediate families who have karmic histories from this life and past lives that include abuse, trauma, alcoholism, and addiction.

The Case of Laura

When I first met my client, Laura, she said, "I have really been feeling stuck lately. Like I am not fulfilling what I have the potential to be doing, and I don't even have the energy to look at what that might be. Overall, my feelings as of late have included frustration, sadness, and a lot of anxiety."

Prior to all my sessions with clients, I go into a slight trance, similar to the method used by Edgar Cayce. I write it all down (with awfully bad handwriting because I am half-asleep!) and report it in the session. In doing this for Laura, it came up very strongly that she had had a past life in an Asian culture and that her current problems had a religious origin. It was clear as day— one of those intuitive "hits" that comes quickly with unmistakable force. I also saw a ring on her finger as a symbol for marriage. I got the impression that there was a breaking of some marriage vows in a past life. When I shared this information with her, it felt like her soul perked up with rabbit ears. She affirmed this impression and said that another psychic had told her that she had broken religious vows in a previous life as well.

As we discussed Asian influences and what they might mean to her, Laura revealed that an Asian woman in her office illogically triggered the worst habitual defenses in her. The woman had done nothing to trigger Laura, and yet she felt a low-grade seething anger toward this woman. Listening to what felt like the urging of Spirit, I asked her if she could engage this woman, get to know her, and perhaps take her out to dinner as a way of completing the cycle and healing the wounds.

To make a long story short, Laura did take the Asian woman out for dinner. Within a few months of establishing a relationship with the person who had prompted so much 'illogical' resentment, Laura found a new job and became engaged to be married to a very sensitive and honorable man. She singlehandedly created a fundraiser for a girl with cancer, began expressing her feelings through painting, attended a Native American sweat lodge, and led a spiritual drum circle on the beach in honor of the new moon.

How did such radical change happen so quickly? I believe it is because she made a concerted effort to eliminate the harmful influences of her past. Instead of ignoring the Shadow, she made a conscious decision to eliminate its influences head on through spiritual therapy and recognizing the truth of what her Highest Self was trying to tell her. She has been rewarded by Spirit for her diligence.

The last I heard from Laura, she stated the following: *"I know that so much of the progress that I have made over the past year has led me here and helped me to be clear and open to listening to God. I know that there are things that I am ready to let go of, things from the past, old ways of being with others, old ways of viewing myself. I have done some more exploring about one of my past lives. I am in the process of breaking a pattern (or perhaps several) that has not only affected me in this life, but in at least one other one as well! That feels really huge! I'm so excited, it makes me emotional just to think about it! I am so ready to be done with so many things from the past."*

Laura is an example of someone who is thriving in Earth's new age. She is also an example of a person who is doing what I call "working it." She's looking hard at her past patterns and habits. She is acknowledging influences that are likely due to past lives or old energies, whatever their origin. Because she's "working it" at the young age of 24, there is little doubt that she will continue to learn new ways of being, to thrive, and achieve her goal of helping others. And because she took the time to be diligent about journaling her experiences, she is now in this book, providing inspiration for others to make similar difficult decisions. She is the "butterfly effect" in action, which will be explored in a following section.

As you read her words and experience her story, what types of reactions do you have about your own life? What things do you need to let go of? What areas of your life have been asking for your attention? How will you move forward, this week, this month, this year, right now, with an urgency to clear the wounds of the past?

Karma is so mysterious that it's absolutely delicious! The old is the new. The new is the old. And if that doesn't make sense, it's because it cannot—at least not yet. At some point it will make sense. Until then, we wait—patient, silent, and still—for the next clue, the next hint, the next mirror to be raised to our eyes, showing us light so that we may see more.

Physician and past-life therapist Dr. Brian Weiss explains that we must be careful about the idea of karma so not as to engage in black and white thinking. Just because you are experiencing a symptom in this lifetime does not necessarily mean that this is punishment for the sins of the past. He states that we don't necessarily agree to be abused or to be victims, but we have agreed to participate in a "certain lesson or type of drama." He says that above all, karma is learning to avoid destructive behavior.

Here's the scoop on our new era: There is only yes. The universe has *never* taken no for an answer. No matter how many bad decisions we've made, individually and collectively, over the course of human history, we get another chance. No matter how much negative karma we've accumulated, we get to vacuum it up. God gives us a Hoover (or does he prefer Eureka?) and asks us to suck up all the energy of bad past decisions.

We are on the brink of something that feels tangible, something that feels BIG. We're getting an opportunity to do this RIGHT. Those who have had near-death experiences and crossed over to the Other Side have much information to share. One of the recurring themes among near-death experiences across cultures, language, time and space, is a belief that everything is for the good. Everything is done for a reason, and no matter how bad our choices were in the past, we get an opportunity to make better decisions later.

That opportunity is now.

In the New Age There Are No Shortcuts

Turn on the television, open any internet web page, or go anywhere there is advertising, and you will be bombarded with messages that trick our egos into believing that there is an easy and quick way to achieve just about anything. These messages usually come from a business or corporation that has a vested interest in our remaining unquestioning and unconscious.

While there is no doubt that achieving our hearts' desires can be easy, the messages in advertising are rarely in harmony with spiritual principles. Although we are on the journey of coming back together, it can still can be disheartening to see so many of our elected officials, corporations, celebrities, and other important people be so out of touch with their hearts.

So many current business practices reflect a belief, borne of Shadow, that shortcuts can be taken in business and industry. For example, farmers long wondered how to achieve higher yields of milk from livestock. Industry's answer was to create an artificial growth hormone that pushes the limits of what nature intends a cow to produce. That same industry ignores significant scientific data showing that these hormones are harmful. *The World According to Monsanto*, and *Food, Inc.* are among an increasing number of documentaries that expose these practices. It has been an unfortunate practice of the food industry to ignore data showing harmful effects, thinking they can override natural law.

Other businesses, including the pharmaceutical industry, have followed a similar pattern of suppression. In his book, *Prozac Backlash,* Physician Dr. Joseph Glenmullen provides a damning indictment that the pharmaceutical industry has suppressed dangerous side effects (which include permanent Parkinsonian-like disorders) of psychiatric drugs such as Zoloft and Prozac.

Even our government leaders are not immune to pursuing profit and cutting corners at the expense of the people. Personal profit, campaign contributions, and pure ambition drive many elected leaders to unethical and illegal behavior. Former senator John Edwards, former Illinois governor Rod Blagojevich, and senator John Ensign are examples of once- esteemed politicians whose unethical and deceptive behavior have been revealed.

In contrast, in many indigenous and Native American traditions, tribal leaders were chosen only after enduring a series of tests. Tribal societies would test their future leaders through seemingly barbaric practices such as burying them in dirt and urinating or defecating near them. These tests were designed to make the candidates stronger and to show them that leadership comes with heavy burdens. Leadership is not to be desired just for power. It is all too common in our ego-driven societies for politicians to chase leadership because it comes with perks of power, fame, and money. All these only serve the small mind.

Unfortunately, many of us have the belief that it is possible to go against natural law—spiritual universal law—in order to achieve our desires. In this new age, sooner rather than later, we will recognize that this is impossible. There was a time when I believed I could cut corners. I thought that pills would help alleviate my physical symptoms. They helped mask symptoms, but I became somewhat addicted, which caused a state of ungrounded fogginess. The resulting numbness turned into a spiritual sickness that led me to make some unhealthy decisions.

The Catholic church believed that by covering up rampant sexual abuse by the clergy, it would go away. They now realize that even the pope, who was silent, perhaps even in denial, for so long, was not immune to the Shadow. The number of lives that have been destroyed because of hiding the painful truth is staggering. In 2010 Pope Benedict XVI met with a group of victims of clerical sex-abuse at the Vatican's embassy in Malta. With tears in his eyes, he told them that the Catholic church would seek justice for pedophile priests and implement measures to protect young people from abuse. The pope's tears and apology are a good start.

Toyota, once world-renowned for making cars of exceptional quality, began to cut corners around 2004. The result was hundreds of crashes and injuries and the deaths of approximately 80 people from problems with unintended and unstoppable acceleration. Their focus on short-term profit ultimately caused extensive damage and suffering.

British Petroleum (BP) was in the headlines in 2010 for one of the worst environmental disasters in modern history—a massive oil spill in the Gulf of Mexico. In their desire to quickly contain the spill, they used chemicals that were revealed to be even more toxic than the original oil spill. This disaster caused a huge amount of suffering among the people—not just in the Gulf region, but in the entire world. Environmental damage to water, wetlands, and wildlife will be felt for decades. I do not believe it was a coincidence that this oil rig disaster happened on the 40th anniversary of Earth Day. I believe that this was another example of Spirit trying hard to get our attention. Curiously, just one week later, a natural gas platform sank in the ocean. The Earth is forcefully attempting, and rightfully so, to shake off those who are literally raping it.

Cutting corners is never effective in business, and it's never effective when dealing with our spiritual life. In this new age, Spirit is demanding that we become aligned with spiritual principles. It is no longer a request. The more we ignore our inner desires, the more we delude ourselves into thinking it's possible to ignore our hearts, the more we will eventually *suffer*. Spirit will no longer tolerate selfish denial borne of a belief that we can remain invisible and that no one will see our self-deception.

Despite the depressing headlines, in our new age some beautiful changes are occurring with business practices. Many businesses are thriving because they are aligned with spiritual principles. They are appearing in unlikely niches, such as marketing and publicity. Andrea Adler is one example. She is the owner of Holistic PR, a company devoted to the promotion of "the science of spiritual marketing," and has written a great book with the same title. This is a positive example of thriving in the new age.

Just like Andrea has found a niche by blending spirituality and marketing, what are the special niches that you can serve? What unique skills do you bring to the table? Is there a way that you can offer a spiritual perspective on a career or skill set that until now has been "off the table" in relation to spiritual principles? There may be a demand for your perspective.

Spirit is waiting for you to take baby steps and foray into the great unknown. You might be surprised, like I was, in choosing to work with empaths and highly sensitive people, at the level of demand for your chosen subject. It is up to each of us to make it our intention to not support individuals, firms, and politicians who do not support spiritual principles. We cannot remain in denial any longer. The Earth requires it. Our Highest Selves are requiring it, and we as a culture are demanding it.

In government, as in business, some positive steps are being taken. Dr. John Hagelin, a renowned physicist who was the presidential candidate of the Natural Law Party in the 1990's, is now president of the American Peace Government. His goal is to help align our Western, European-centric government with spiritual principles, including quantum physics, in which he received a doctorate degree. Regardless of what you think of his politics, there is little doubt that he is fulfilling his mission on Earth. I am not advocating this political philosophy. Rather, we recognize this governmental and political shift for what it is: reflections of a world that has been "split" and is now coming back together.

Exercise: Declaration of Independence From Cutting Corners

1. Ask yourself the question, What are the areas of my life where I have cut corners? Let your awareness float. Scope the insides and outsides of your body, mind, and spirit. Ask yourself if you have guilt about any of your behaviors. The feeling of guilt is sometimes there to ask us to change our patterns of behavior.

2. Resolve to make a commitment, firm and unwavering, that you will no longer support cutting corners.

3. Take out a sheet of paper. Write the words: "On this day, I declare my independence   from   _____   and   commit   instead   to _____."

4. Place this declaration on your refrigerator or on your desk. Distribute copies to partners and members of your family.

5. Ask your family members and support system to help hold you accountable to following through on this declaration.

6. To take it further, every time you follow the pledge, reinforce your behavior by rewarding yourself in a small way.

Exercise: Seeing Yourself With the Eyes of God

Here's one of my favorite guided meditations. If we're stuck in one way of viewing ourselves, this exercise can give us a new perspective. It can quickly shift old beliefs and rearrange the furniture inside us! This exercise also leads to self-compassion, which is often all we   need   to   get   us   moving   in   the   right   direction.

1. Take several deep oxygenating breaths. An oxygenating breath is one that is approximately 10 seconds on the inhale, and 10 seconds on the exhale. The extra oxygen promotes blood and energy circulation. This is a type of breathing that you learn if you practice yoga.

2. Roll your shoulders gently back in their sockets. This has the effect of opening the chest.

3. Transfer your consciousness out of your head and into your heart chakra.

4. Pretend your heart has a mouth.

5. Say hello to your heart. Offer it gratitude for protecting you and helping you remain alive. Tell it that you are wanting to engage in a dialogue.

6. Ask your heart, How does God see me? Notice the images that arise.

7. Ask your heart, How does God feel me? Notice the feelings in your body.

8. Ask your heart, How does God hear me? Notice the sounds that come.

I Don't Know and I Don't Need to Know

There was a time when I was convinced that the world in which we live, with its rigid social structures, would "end." Because I was having daily and nightly visions of earthquakes, I, like many, dutifully prepared for massive changes. In 2007, I asked my mother for a curious holiday gift: seeds. Happy to oblige, she sent away for mail order seeds. Those seeds are still there, just in case.

However, that's not what I'm focused on these days. Whether or not our electrical grids will cease to function is not my concern. To quote one of my favorite phrases, which has become a full-fledged spiritual practice: *I don't know and I don't need to know*. Part, if not all, of navigating our way around the new age involves surrendering—not just to ourselves, but surrendering to our *need to know*.

Coming from the world of academia, with all its trappings, I had previously believed the following myth: *I know and I think I know*. Giving up a need to know is medicine for the soul. It assuages the ego with its desire for total control, total knowledge, and attempting to master that which is impossible for it to understand. Make it your practice to use *'I don't know and I don't need to know'* as a mantra. You may be pleasantly surprised at how liberating it is to say those words with total conviction.

Remembering the Future, Creating the Past

Everything that you have ever wanted to do, on a soul level, has already been done. Time is an illusion and does not exist in realms other than the Earth. In this new age it is time to chip away at the rock and uncover your creations that are already there, just like Michelangelo uncovered his.

Your poems are written. Your songs are written. Your ideal partner is already there, waiting for you to evolve spiritually to match his or her vibration. Your talents have already produced the masterful works of art at which you so excel. Your gifts at communication and persuasion have already brought about the social change that will help countless thousands. Your unique listening skills have already allowed people to overcome their struggles with heartache, disillusionment, addictions, and emotional relapse.

This process is called "Remembering the Future." You ask for information from your Highest Self about Who You Are. Over time, if you work hard enough and show Spirit that you mean business, you receive clues. You will receive gifts from Spirit through symbols, dreams, feelings, and memories.

You only need to ask, and then let go of any control over how the messages and clues come to you. Over time you will receive visions, clues, and synchronicities that will allow you to recognize yourself in the experiences in which you immerse yourself. You will begin to realize that all your feelings, dreams, and yearnings have a common thread: they are simply "memories." From where, exactly, do they originate? Asking yourself that question will keep you searching, walking down the path of life, and uncovering new experiences until the moment you take your last breath. And then, too, another portion of the Great Mystery will be revealed.

"Creating the Past" is prayer from the heart to erase bad decisions we've made previously. From a psychokinetic standpoint, the intention itself is enough to alter space and time. We ask that any unfortunate decisions of the past be healed and that better future decisions be made in those past moments. How these past experiences are healed we don't know. We give up all sense of control. And yet, when I pray in this way, I know beyond a shadow of a doubt that these experiences are changing because I experience evidence of this. I feel lighter when I pray this way. I feel changed. My heart opens.

I will often pray that my 1989 self makes better decisions so that his future will be brighter. Or that the 1968 Richard Nixon makes better decisions so that the country and world may not have to suffer. Since time is happening all at once, the 1968 Richard Nixon could fundamentally be altered by your decision to pray for him now! And perhaps the Vietnam war, or even the suffering caused by the Watergate saga, can be erased, "rolled back" in the eyes of God. Your prayers for Richard Nixon could cause our current experience to become lighter, freer, and less full of experiences that run contrary to the nature of God.

Is that mind-blowing? If so, good, because that's what the Divine is aiming for!

Exercise: Creating the Past

1. Connect with a time in your life when you were confused or lost.

2. Pray to that person that you were previously. Create a feeling of love in your heart. Ask that this love be sent to yourself at that time.

3. Ask that the past, which is occurring in other dimensions, be "erased." Ask that you make better decisions at that time, coming from a place of greater love and awareness.

4. When this exercise is done repeatedly from a strong heart, your prayer may create enough critical mass to allow psychokinetic shifts to occur. Your current experience may become lighter because of your prayers

Chaos

For centuries scientists sought to understand the world through what they believed to be a principle of evolution that operated in a linear fashion: cause and effect. Recently, however, with the advent of quantum physics, we have realized that things are not always what they seem. Increasingly, there is the awareness that living organisms and societies are much more fluid and dynamic in their evolution. This, in short, is what Chaos Theory is all about.

Personally, I enjoy Chaos Theory. (I had the fortunate "coincidence" to be trained by the only two social scientists in my field, at separate institutions and years apart, who were applying Chaos Theory to group counseling behavior. Many thanks to Bud McClure for stimulating my interest at the University of Minnesota and to Edil Torres-Rivera for refining it at the University of Nevada-Reno during my doctoral studies.) But if you're one of the souls among us who have no time or patience for science, especially for lofty terms such as Chaos Theory, you're probably asking yourself what your motivation would be to continue reading this chapter.

Here's a short reason why: You are a strange attractor!

A strange attractor is anything that influences the larger system—in this case, the entire universe and all of creation. By continuing to read this book, perhaps you'll be stimulated by the ideas enough that you will make one small change in your behavior. And perhaps it will be significant enough that you'll do it right now, or within the next hour.

You will most likely be unaware of the effect of your actions on the entire system, and yet your actions, however small, could be the deciding factor in whether humanity moves into one path versus the other. According to philosopher and systems theorist Ervin Lazlo, Chaos Theory teaches us that the world, and everything in it (e.g., you) oscillate between periods of stability and instability. Fairly routinely, we go back and forth between these poles of existence, sometimes stable, sometimes unstable. Every now and then we make a discontinuous "leap" and evolve into something completely unexpected. According to Ervin Lazlo, humanity is at a point of such massive change.

No one can know the day, the hour, or the moment when this will occur. To put it another way, using the famous excerpt from Matthew 24:36 in the *Bible*, "No one knows about that day or hour, not even the angels in heaven." This moment, whenever it occurs, will depend on how each of us moves. One seemingly insignificant move by you can influence much larger collective individuals or systems. This is the so-called "butterfly effect," and it has important ramifications.

So, by making the decision to continue reading this chapter, you could cause an an earthquake in Japan, a social uprising in Thailand, or who knows? The possibilities are Infinite. You could be the deciding factor as to whether humanity goes down a path of destruction or evolves into a species that lives in harmony with the universe. According to Ervin Lazlo, when "a society turns chaotic, it becomes supersensitive, responsive to even small fluctuations, such as changes in the values, beliefs, worldviews, and aspirations of its members."

Perhaps you didn't realize you had that much power?

This is why it's so important for us to continue our personal and collective evolution. By moving forward with determined integrity, we will help, literally, to change the world.

God sees this. Over time, so will we.

Entrainment

Chaos Theory also teaches us about entrainment. This word describes what indigenous people know occurs when people are together in ceremony. We move together. Literally. Entrainment is one of the quickest ways to move up spiritually. If you are exposed to a certain frequency long enough, you eventually change your vibration to match the frequency to which you are exposed. This happens in interpersonal relationships, in student-teacher relationships, in the workplace, in every interaction in the world. The more you know about entrainment, the better you will be prepared to change others to *your* frequency rather than let them change you to their negative frequencies.

Entrainment is the mechanism that allows the Law of Attraction to work. The Law of Attraction has been popularized by bestselling books such as *The Secret* and lesser-known but brilliant books such as *Excuse Me, Your Life is Waiting: The Astonishing Power of Feelings* by Lynn Grabhorn.

Says Grabhorn about the practical uses of entrainment for attracting what we want: "State your wants every day. And pretend. Get into the feeling place of what you're pretending, and become the one who is so aggressively flowing your own energy and vibrating in the frequency of joy that you override all that you—or anyone else—might have been flowing before."

An illustrative example of entrainment is when women live in close proximity to one another for sustained periods of time. Their menstrual clocks synchronize and begin to tick in unison. The ability for individuals to move together is also evident in history.

At various times, history-shaping ideas have evolved from scientists who were working on the same projects "independently" of each other. Nikola Tesla and Guglielmo Marconi were working on the same devices to harness the power of electricity for wireless transmission of messages. (Without their contributions, you likely would not be reading this book!) Their work is an example of entrainment. Both scientists may have been altering their frequencies to tune into the universal field to access information and ideas. In fact, without realizing it, they may have been matching their own frequencies, psychically spurring the other on to more growth, more discoveries, and greater understanding.

In order to have our own history-changing "eureka" moments, each of us needs others to help us along in our evolution. Self-help author Stuart Wilde, author of the folksy and informative *Sixth Sense*, says that we need the equivalent of a "starter pistol" to get over the hump. We can't do it alone. We need critical mass in order to move forward. The "starter pistol" is other people congregating in large groups to move energy and entrain together. This can be done through a variety of practices, such as the Native American sweat lodge ceremony, or through stadium events like the Qi Revolution (qigong.com) where large numbers of people breathe in prana energy and entrain their vibrations together for healing purposes.

Our ventures into the spiritual universe, seeking spiritual growth with our magnifying glasses, must be done in conjunction with other people. If we are isolated, afraid, in our houses and scared to go outside, it will be difficult to experience the effects of community entrainment. Many highly sensitive people experience symptoms of agoraphobia. Because they have been entrained in the past to harmful lower vibratory frequencies, they assume that staying home and becoming detached is the only solution.

The more you actively seek your spiritual power (described in the next chapter) and engage in a community spiritual practice, along with the counsel of a spiritual mentor, the more you will entrain others to your positive frequency. People will want to be around you even more, and you will bring more abundance and joy into the world.

In the New Age There Are Earthquakes—of Many Kinds

Recently, in a span of one week, on separate occasions, three clients reported being disturbed by dreams and visions of massive earthquakes. One reported a premonition of "the big one" occurring in California. Another saw a tsunami in California. These were in addition to three other friends who reported dreams and premonitions of earthquakes.

Such visions are nothing new. Native and indigenous wisdom keepers have been talking about Earth changes for years. The urgency with which you may be receiving visions and messages may seem new to you because it is only now, because of the higher vibration on the planet, that we are able to break through the barriers of the ego. Nothing is coming from you alone. It's all part of the bigger picture, what native societies call the "web of life." The web is a useful representation of how we are all connected. The web is just another word for God. You can take comfort in the realization that if you are receiving messages and wisdom in your dreams or through intuition, it is very likely that others are as well.

Just as the Earth is changing, so are we. We are experiencing earthquakes just like the Earth, although ours are psychic and emotional. Our psychic earthquakes jolt us into the realization that we are not alone. Each of us must take serious responsibility for the creation of our new age and new world. Even President Barack Obama alluded to this, although perhaps with a different intention, with his famous phrase "the fierce urgency of now."

In order to propel us into new dimensions, we need the equivalent of an earthquake to get us over the hump. In Chaos Theory, this is called the bifurcation point. This is the point at which we are propelled into dramatic change through a series of small actions that build into a critical mass tipping point. Something is indeed happening *now.*

That's why it's imperative that we learn about our abilities and gifts, enroll in healing classes, and go to spiritual ceremonies. We don't have any time left to remain in avoidance, denial, separation, or ignorance! The time is now. We've got no other choice.

If and when Earth changes or other disasters happen, we need to be the ones to remain calm in the center of the storm and have already honed our abilities to help others. (This is one reason why I have created an empath and highly sensitive person scholarship program). The point is that you do something, anything, other than what you've been doing. Any moment can be the tipping point.

Technology as a Reflection of the Ascension

Every time you post a status update on Facebook are you tapping into the Great Mind? What about Twitter? Are your 140-character posts a reflection of the Ascension? Are you not allowing others to hear your intimate thoughts, feelings, and desires just the way God does? When viewed in this perspective, we see that technology is allowing us to tap into each others' thoughts in a way we have never been able to before. In a way, it is like telepathy.

And yet our nervous systems sometimes can't keep up with the advances. Part of learning to navigate our way through the new age involves downtime, honoring when we become overwhelmed with input. In the process of writing this book, as a means to cope with stress over self-imposed deadlines, I decided not to respond to email for one day. It was a lot harder than I thought it would be, but it allowed me to experience just how caught up we can become in other people's stories! Reading the Huffington Post, monitoring Twitter, and constant Facebook updates can interfere with the silence required to receive messages from our Highest Self. We want to take the time to engage silence as a means of handling new stresses. Rightful balance in our relationship with technology will allow us to be more fully present and aware of important spiritual data and messages that come our way.

In the New Age We Have Balance Between Polarities

Navigating around the new age involves acknowledging that everything in the universe exists between two poles—heaven and Earth, black and white, heavy and light, male and female. A life lived well is a life in which we are ideally balanced between the reception, perception, and expression of various poles of energy. At any moment you may ask how best to exist in a state of balance between heart and mind. Will you allow yourself the grace and permission to flow freely back and forth between the expression of your masculine nature and your feminine nature, regardless of what biological sex you are? Is your right hand stronger than your left? Perhaps you may seek to make the left stronger.

It is helpful for the small mind, the ego, to understand that these navigations between poles are a large part of moving effortlessly through our new spiritual age. The goal of this age is to return to an awareness that everything in the universe is part of the One. There is a phrase that goes, "As above, so as below," which means that everything, no matter how small, is a reflection of the whole. An ant is a reflection of God. We must not focus on the small to the detriment of the large. We must not ignore the large because we are only focused on the small. We do not want to get lost and not see the forest because we are focused on the trees. Balance is key.

Our understanding of polarities is framed by paradox. To have one, we cannot *not* have the other. To have light, we must have dark. To have masculine, we must have feminine. Polarities exist not within a framework, but *despite* the framework. Despite our best attempts to locate one without the other, or one within the other, or one in relation to the other, our Highest Selves know that there is no separation, no duality. As humans, we experience both sides of the coin—the heads and the tails.

Here are just some of the polarities:

Male and Female
Heavy and Light
Fire and Ice
Hot and Cold.
Large and Small..
Left and Right
Inside and Out
Top and Bottom
Eagle and Mouse
Push and Pull
Negative and Positive
Mother Earth and Father Sky
Empty and Full
Inhale and Exhale
Contraction and Expansion
Big and Small
Vague and Precise
Intuition and Intellect

In many yogic and indigenous traditions, the space in between the polarities is described as the place where God resides. In other words, we find God in the neutral place between polarities. The space in between the in breath and the out breath is the place of ecstasy and the place of enlightenment. This is the place of divine balance.

At some point in your spiritual development ask for the experience of neutrality. It may seem awkward and even downright uncomfortable, especially if you're used to being expansive and spiritually enthusiastic. Being in a neutral place, which can manifest as a feeling of not really caring deeply about anything, is actually one of the best places to be in order to advance your intuition. It is the place where infinite possibilities are born. When you are in a place of neutrality, you are experiencing yourself and the world for what it is. You are not biased, reacting, or projecting. You are truly centered when you can be in this state of neutrality. Be careful not to equate a feeling of detached neutrality with a loss of passion. They are not one and the same.

There's a time and a place for passion (in the bedroom or in the boardroom when creativity is needed). However, you cannot be passionate at all times or you will become unbalanced. Some astrological signs like Aquarius and Sagittarius might find this notion difficult because they are ruled by planets whose inclinations are for expansion. On the other hand, earthly signs that are ruled by Saturn, such as Capricorn, or other Earth signs like Virgo are blessed with energies of contraction and reserve. This can be extremely helpful, yet it can lead to lack of passion when you are out of balance. There are no absolutes. The key word is balance!

END With Love

Whenever we are faced with a stimulus, we have a choice in how to react based on the three responses explained below. END stands for the following choices:

E = Engage
N = Neutral
D = Disengage

END is a mnemonic device that helps you remember that you always have a choice as to how you will react to a stimulus. Whatever you choose, you do it out of love. "END with Love" helps us examine our reactions in order to promote better balance.

On the spectrum of engagement, END markers could mean many things. For example, engagement of others could mean disengagement from oneself. The universe has given us free will as to how we handle our affairs. And yet an important task to master is the following: whatever choice you do make, you do it out of love. If you choose to engage, you do it out of love. If you choose to remain neutral, you do it out of love. And if you disengage, you do it out of love. For too long we have chosen our behaviors out of the opposite of love—fear. All behaviors born of fear are detrimental. They do not produce results that move us forward in our spiritual growth.

Let's take our typical response to stress as an example. Most of us, when faced with stressful situations, tend to favor one of the responses on the END spectrum over the other. In your interpersonal relationships, what has been your default state? For instance, do you disengage from your partner when faced with his or her stress? Or do you over-engage to the point of losing yourself?

Many people vacillate between the extremes of over-engagement to pacify a situation and disengagement to prevent being hurt or experiencing negativity. Do you recognize yourself in one of these END markers? Do you have a habitual response to stress? If you do, just remember that your responses are nothing more than learned behaviors.

In these new times, with our new responsibilities, we want to examine our behavioral patterns and ask, How can I function optimally? How can I exist in a state of balance between my responsibilities for myself and my responsibilities for others? Am I functioning at an optimal energetic state? If not, what do I desire to engage to raise my energy?

This might take the form of volunteering to promote engagement with your community. Or you might engage your physical self and start an exercise plan. What might you disengage from in order to preserve energy? This might take the form of setting limits to the conversations you have with those who drain your energy. It might involve creating tighter boundaries around what you are willing to do for loved ones or friends, especially those that are feeding off your engagement. Is your engagement creating a distraction from experiencing your *own* experience? If so, how do you disengage?

Remember, the universe only takes yes for an answer. So no matter what choice you make, do it with love. Simply create a feeling of love in your heart and move forward, empowered, with your choice.

Polarity Exercise #1: Examine your Eyes and Face For Polarity Markers

One way to see how your body and nervous system deal with energy input and output is to examine the small differences in individuals between the left and right eyes. Many systems of indigenous medicine, including Chinese and Ayurvedic medicine, believe that the left side of the body is feminine and the right side of the body is masculine. This correlates to scientific understanding of the differences between brain hemispheres, with the more feminine and intuitive right brain controlling the left side of the body and the more masculine and linear left brain controlling the right side of the body. As a fun experiment, get out an old photo album and look at the differences in expression between the polarities as it shows up on the faces of individuals.

I have an unsubstantiated theory, supported only by anecdotal observations. I've noticed that shamans, intuitives and people who display extraordinary talent in any particular domain (mental, spiritual, physical, etc.), have a distinct difference in the shape, movement, and expression between their left and right eyes. Sometimes this will pervade the entire side of the face. This difference between the two halves, I

believe, reveals that the person has two personalities—one controlled by
the left brain and one controlled by the right brain. Differences in facial
expressions may reflect that the person has a strong presence in both
worlds simultaneously (e.g., using both halves of the brain for different
tasks).

Get out a piece of paper and an old photo album or set of photos
of yourself and your family members. Take the piece of paper and cover
one half of your face in a photo so that only one side is showing. Notice
the quality of the eye. Then do the same, covering the other side of the
face. You may notice slight differences. If you search long enough, you
will eventually find a picture of yourself where the differences between
your left and right eyes are pronounced. Ask yourself, 'what does this
mean for how my body handles energy?'

Since the left eye correlates to the right hemisphere of the brain,
which controls creativity and intuition, what are the implications for how
you engage that side of the brain? Since the right eye correlates to the
left brain, which controls the linear, mathematical, precise, ego-based
side of our personality, what does that reveal about how much time you
spend in that part of your personality? Do you want to create more
balance? Or are the differences (or lack thereof) reflective of a healthy
ability to exist in both the right and left hemispheres simultaneously?

Polarity Exercise #2: Moving the Eyes For Balance

Our eyes dart back and forth during each night's sleep. This is the
REM, or rapid eye movement phase of sleep. When these eye
movements are reproduced in clinical settings in a psychological
treatment process known as EMDR, trauma is often erased and a feeling
of equilibrium is restored. You can do these eye movements on your
own, especially if you would like to change unwanted emotional or
mental states. Conjure up unwanted emotions or thoughts. Then try a
series of 1-minute eye movements. To do this, move your eyes rapidly, a)
left-right, and b) top-down.

After moving your eyes like this for 1 minute, notice how it changes your energy in the rest of your body. You may feel more balanced, peaceful, and calm.

Chapter Three

Finding Your Spiritual Power,
Healing Yourself, and Moving Forward to the Light

Thinking about your life story, what would it mean to thrive? How would you feel if you were rip-roaringly going after your life's ambition? What would your life look like if you were truly engaged in the pursuits of your heart, your deepest soul-level intentions? How would you treat people? How would they react to you? Would you be giving warm, loving embraces and surrounding your heart and those of others with sheer poetry? Or would you be beholden to the deceit, the lies, the unholy truth of the Shadow? Would you still be stuck in the notion that you are somehow "less than" or unworthy?

As we learn how to navigate our way around in this new terrain, climbing the mountain until we reach the pinnacle of consciousness, our answers to these questions will inform where we arrive as a society and as global humanity. The trajectory of consciousness is being altered. Despite our defenses, in spite of ourselves, we are being moved. The best metaphor I ever heard was that even if you are moving backwards on a moving train, you're still going to get to your destination.

So where are we going? And who is doing the moving?

In the last chapter we explored the state of equilibrium between two poles. Learning to navigate around the new age is largely about learning to exist in two worlds simultaneously. In *Sixth Sense*, Stuart Wilde explores this, describing a series of "hovering maneuvers" for going back and forth between heaven and Earth. Many of us are what some native people refer to as a "walks-between." We can walk our consciousness up to the heavens and bring wisdom back to Earth. You may be asking your Highest Self, How can I exist on Earth in a state that is in union with my Highest Self? You are wanting to maintain equilibrium between two powerful forces: those of heaven and those of Earth. How successful we are depends largely on how we are able to navigate back and forth in a continual series of energetic motions.

Medicine people and shamans have mastered this ability. They are able to move effortlessly between the upper world (heavens) and the lower world (Earth). They can do this because they are rigorous about keeping themselves clean and practicing techniques that allow them to vibrate at a high rate.

In order to keep ourselves energetically clear so that we can receive proper communication between heaven and Earth and broadcast clear signals and receive clear responses, we have to do what the great medicine man Fools Crow calls being a "hollow bone." We must clear ourselves of past energies that lodge in our body's cells over time, sometimes causing illness and disease.

We must be firm in our gentleness toward others and toward God and not let anything distract us from our determination to be clear and clean so that we may be a healing presence and catalyst for others.

Do you think of yourself as a healer? If you don't, why not? Everyone in the world has the ability to heal themselves and heal others. It only requires psychokinesis—mind over matter—a universal spiritual principle that everyone can access. I believe this was the message of Jesus' life and healing ministry: "These things I do, so too can you do." Part of the new age is knowing, deep in your heart, that you are Divine. You have healing abilities, no matter what your small mind may tell you. You have spiritual gifts to offer the world, energies to share, and a shining warm heart that can light up a room.

It's true that you can be a "medicine person." The only requirement is that you be disciplined about practicing your spiritual program. It's what I call "working it," which is similar to AA's program. If you've never been to an AA meeting, *go*. It's a spiritually-oriented program, and you don't have to be alcoholic or have an addiction to benefit from the beauty present in the room where people share their stories (often through tears) of how they are humbling themselves in order to be better people. The power of the medicine of AA and similar 12-step programs is that it is based in community and rooted in the knowledge that all addictions are spiritual in nature (e.g., have spiritual origins and spiritual solutions). "Full-throttle spiritual living" is the term

I give to what many of us are doing.

Here's my brief life story, which I told more fully in my first book, *The Complete Empath Toolkit.* For most of my life I walked around with what felt like several fishing hooks in my chest. My chest always felt blocked and tense. Any time I was touched in that area I had a severe psychic and bodily reaction. I never felt at home in my body. Most empaths have similar feelings since we tend to accumulate other people's energies. If you've ever been told that you are a good listener, or that people feel better after talking to you, you are likely an empath, which is explored more fully in the next chapter.

As a result of being an unskilled and unconscious empath, processing other people's energies for them, my rock bottom occurred when I attempted suicide in the early 2000's. I closed the garage, got in the car, rolled up the windows, started the engine, and fully expected to go Home to the Other Side. I just couldn't take the physical pain any longer. However, my spiritual guides and angels had a different plan for me. The car was still running 8 hours later when I woke up, and I was deflated to find I was still alive. The pain that caused me to attempt to take my own life was not my own. Years of taking on other people's stuff, along with my own past karma, resulted in an explosive mix of emotion that bordered on temporary insanity.

The day after being literally saved from death, I decided it was time to do something about getting clean and clear. So I signed up for a week-long spiritual retreat in the mountains of Santa Fe, New Mexico. It was there that I met my first spiritual mentor, Wolf Martinez, a gifted shaman, mentor, and practitioner of Native American healing arts. Life was not the same after that retreat. There I learned that I needed to "come back" to the circle. I soon started traveling from Laramie, Wyoming, to Santa Fe. I did this, attending sweat lodges on a regular basis, for several years.

Through this experience I realized there was no turning back. In 2005, I quit my lucrative, cushy job as a tenure-track assistant professor of counseling and moved to Santa Fe on a wing and a prayer. I was in search of something more than the left-brain world of academia that was frying the inner recesses of my mind. I had seen a bumper sticker that said "Leap and the Net Will Appear." With no job prospects to speak of, I placed my trust in believing that all the right things would appear. They did. I followed the flicker of light in my heart that things could be better.

Over the course of the next several years I went full throttle. I endured ceremony after ceremony where I felt like a complete fool and sweat lodge after intense sweat lodge where old energies got cleansed. I was humbled by my experiences. I needed to be humbled. In doing this, Spirit showered me with gifts. I expanded and became a more vibrant being.

In Santa Fe I picked up a degree in polarity therapy from the New Mexico Academy of Healing Arts. I started working on and off the body, and explored for the first time what it felt like to be grounded in my body. I started traveling and expanded my lifelong interest in dancing, movement, and yoga. I traveled to Asia and spent a month hiking through rural villages. I shared a bottle of hallucinogenic moonshine with a tribal chief in one memorable encounter. I started attending ceremonies in world religions: Buddhism, dharma talks, Japanese tea ceremony, Sufi Zikr, and African trance-dance. I spent a summer living in a tent on a hill at the Lama Foundation in Taos, New Mexico, where I met Mark, who included part of my life story in a book he was writing, *If Buddha Were a Texan*. I still laugh at how he described me as a half-crazy professor who was junking his education to live more freely and go "deeper."

I became good friends with psychics and healers. I got my hair cut every month from Jaoquin Torres, a high priest in Santeria, and in the process learned about African ways of healing (The African Spirit of Oya subsequently appeared to me.). I bought a drum and attended drum ceremonies, learning that the drum reflects the precise emotional and mental state we are in. My earnest steps were being rewarded through medicine dreams and astral voyages. I started working with channeling, befriending an experienced channel in Santa Fe. And much to my surprise, the angels started speaking to me. All this occurred in a few years' time. Time is a spirit, and your relationship with it will influence not only your perception of how fast it moves, but also how you age.

A wise mentor, Edil Torres Rivera, a counseling professor at the University of Nevada, who himself worked closely with Native Americans and planted the seed for my doing so, once asked a group of counselors, "How far are you willing to go in order to be good?"

It's a question that each of us must face at some point in our lives, and the universe may now be posing it to you. Many of us are being asked to go farther than others. Our hearts are being tugged at on a soul level. If God suddenly appeared and spoke those words into your heart, what would you say? How would you respond to the call? It is my hope and prayer that you would keep going forward, no matter what the perceived cost, no matter how hard or even unrealistic it may seem.

I kept going in my darkest days of physical and emotional pain because something was becoming activated inside me. My soul was coming to the surface, just like what is happening now for many of us. I knew I had important things to do with my life. I had important messages to share. I had an important role to play, just like you, just like many of my clients, whose stories I am privileged to share in the hopes that you may be inspired by their courage and conviction.

Janice

My client, Janice, was a 42-year-old businesswoman with a lucrative career. She was an information technology officer in a large corporation when she suffered a brain aneurysm. She was declared clinically dead three times on the operating table and had what is called a "near-death experience." (The Near Death Experience Research Foundation has collected hundreds of thousands of reports similar to Janice's.) During the time she was "dead," she crossed over and spoke with angels, specifically with the energies of Archangel Michael and Archangel Gabriel. They gave her messages that she was to bring back into her life in order to heal.

When Janice came to me for counseling, she was only a month removed from the trauma of her bleeding brain and physical death. She was like a wobbly deer taking its first steps. We worked to validate her experiences and affirm her intuition. She began to see how the intense pressure of being in a job she didn't like was partially responsible for the rupture in her brain. We worked on slowing her life down, getting in touch with her intuitive side, and doing everything possible to gain confidence in her abilities. She was exceptionally gifted as an intuitive. As I do with many clients, I offer to be their "client" for practice in using their intuitive abilities. She was astoundingly accurate with her perceptions of what was happening with me, physically and emotionally.

She was soon rewarded for her courage. Through the grace of her own determined spirit, she came back to Earth for a reason—to teach and help others. Within a year she had transitioned out of her soulless job and set up shop as a psychic counselor. She started small, doing readings for a few clients. Then she gained confidence in not only her abilities, but in how good it made her feel to be fulfilling her mission and engaging in the career of her heart. Now she facilitates spiritual seminars in Los Angeles, even mingling with celebrities and teaching spiritual principles to those in situations much like her former work situation. Janice is an example of thriving in Earth's new age.

You too, can thrive. It takes is a sustained effort over time, with prayer and intention from your heart of hearts. It may involve facing your fears. Spirit sees your courage and willingness. You will be rewarded with a new you.

Becoming a Hollow Bone and Learning About Our Own Medicine

In his excellent book, *Fools Crow: Wisdom and Power,* Thomas Mails, a white man, was allowed to capture the beliefs of one of the most sacred Native American Sioux holy men, Fools Crow. Through a series of interviews, Fools Crow explained how spiritual power works. Medicine people think of themselves as hollow tubes or "hollow bones" through which spiritual power flows. Medicine people go through cleansing rituals to remove all doubt or fear that would impede healing. Then they are able to experience power as it comes surging into them and give the power away in the knowledge that as they are emptied out, Higher Powers will keep filling them with even greater power to be given away.

Fools Crow describes what many of us have been experiencing. "Some people think we are chosen for this while we are still in our mother's womb," he said. "We have strange feelings, and we think about the Higher Powers more than other children do. We go apart and contemplate what is happening to us." Fools Crow says that God, Wakan-Tanka, sees that. "It is like we have bodies that are covered with holes through which they enter and fill us, and out of which our prayers and desires go up to them."

He also says that medicine people must "forego many of the ordinary pleasures of life." We have a responsibility to others as spiritually sensitive people. If we hear our intuition, if we are connected to Spirit, if we have felt different from other people since birth, then we likely are medicine people with healing gifts to share. That means that we have a responsibility to ourselves and others to make ourselves fresh, clean, and sparkly. We are meant to be happy, to thrive, to communicate, to exchange energy with others. We are not meant to be isolated.

We're all asking to be medicine people in the new age. We are asking to share our unique gifts with the world. We all carry the energy of God within us. Inside your cells, the quivering containers for the divine, down to the smallest parts of your being, you know *where you are going*. For all eternity.

It may not always be apparent. Yet with a little light shown in the right places at the right time, your Highest Self will lead you to a destination, a state of being that contains wisdom and truth. We're being asked to go to that place, that energy, that power - for the renewal of our galaxy and its inhabitants, for our animal brethren including the snakes, the snow leopards, the ants—for the faeries, for soldiers and politicians, for all things "real" and "imagined."

Mirror Exercise:

Look at yourself in the mirror. Ask yourself, Who am I? Stare at your skin. See if you can look past the skin to go deeper. Notice every edge, every contour of your skin. Keep asking yourself, Who am I? This exercise promotes a feeling of depersonalization in which you become psychically loosened from the grip that your ego has on you. You may have interesting experiences with the mirror exercise if you allow yourself to fully sink into the experience.

Finding a Spiritual Community

Healing the circle is ideally done in conjunction with others. We must rely on each other to transmute darkness for each other. I believe that we are returning to small, intimate, communal, perhaps tribally influenced ways of living together. If climate change and Earth changes continue in the manner in which they have been occurring, those who are isolated will probably not survive. We are being asked to come back to the circle, and to come back to the whole. At some point it may no longer be a request. It may indeed become a requirement for survival.

Finding a spiritual community can take many forms, from finding an embracing and accepting church. (Unity churches and Center for Spiritual Living churches are two denominations that practice metaphysical principles.) Or perhaps you prefer to gather with friends and loved ones in someone's home.

The Omega Institute in New York, Kripalu in Massachusetts, and the Esalen Institute in California are renowned examples of intentional spiritual communities that offer healing through pooling consciousness. A lesser known example, but just as powerful, is the Lama Foundation near Taos, New Mexico. I was blessed to spend a summer there in 2005. I lived in a tent on the side of the hill and helped grow organic vegetarian food. Every summer the organization expands its numbers to offer summer internships and workshops. Living in intentional spiritual community may be the model for survival in the coming years.

Embracing Sexuality

And now for the subject that terrifies many of us: sex.

There is much *fertility* around this subject. It is rich to explore the true power contained in the sexual chakras and sexual acts themselves.

One of the best viral emails I ever received contained a rant from a woman who only identified herself as Victoria. The question was about how to best ground oneself. Forget all the visualizations and other techniques, she said. Simply have an orgasm. There's nothing better, she advocated.

Unfortunately, many in our Western culture would prefer to keep frank discussion of sexuality in the dark. In doing so, we can ignore our root chakras and become disconnected from the powerful kundalini energy contained in orgasms. It means that we sometimes turn our backs on a whole class of people—gay, lesbian, and transgendered individuals.

These are examples of our denial about the Shadow and confusing the Shadow with sexuality. Sexuality is one of the most powerful and natural aspects of being human. Far too many people in Western society have cut themselves off from their sexual power. In doing so, they cut themselves off from Creator, from God, from Source energy. Reclaiming your personal power means being fully sexual without shame.

Sexual power might be the greatest power on Earth, next to love and gratitude. Sex is one of the best ways to become grounded and can be the quickest way to attain connection with the spirit world. Before many traditional Native American ceremonies, the initiate is required to go a certain amount of time (often 4, 7, or 30 days) without any form of sexual act.

In South America, those training to become shamans (often referred to as "curanderos") will also withhold themselves from sexual stimulation of any kind. This is so that sexual energy can be preserved—not "spill the seed" as the *Bible* says. This means that we are not careless in using our sexual energy. We hold and nurture our sexual and spiritual powers, slowly and surely building them up from the root chakra. The origin of why priests are required to be celibate in the Catholic church is rooted in the human experience that holding one's sexual energy allows the cultivation of a higher vibration and easier access to the higher realms.

In many Native American traditions, women are not allowed to enter most ceremonies when they are on their "moon time." At first I thought this was misogynous. Only later did I come to see that it was quite the opposite. A woman's sexual power is at her strongest when she is menstruating. To have that much power present in the ceremony can often be overwhelming for everyone. That's why there are special ceremonies for women who are on their moon time.

The most effective healers, priests, psychics, and shamans are deeply in touch with the power of the feminine, and this is why many indigenous societies have chosen gay and lesbian individuals as tribal healers. These individuals are considered "two-spirits" who have equal parts male and female, and thus can access sexual power more freely. Early in my training, my mentor made me wear a dress during spiritual ceremony in order to harness female power and to be more deeply in touch with my own two-spirited nature.

Harnessing female power is about moving slowly, quietly, and deliberately. It is about harnessing the power contained in Tai Chi, in which strength is acquired through slow movements. When your awareness is outside of your head, which is considered masculine by many systems of indigenous medicine, then you are in the female power of being, which is slower and quieter.

Males can harness their sexual power as well. Men can actually have multiple orgasms. Thousands of years ago the Chinese recognized that orgasm and ejaculation in the male are separate processes. They also discovered, and science has backed this up, that sperm creation is a complex, energetically draining process.

Vitality can be increased through holding back and cultivating sexual energy. If you're male, you can learn about this in the book *The Multi-Orgasmic Man: Sexual Secrets Every Man Should Know*. The authors state that "creating sperm is far more difficult than scientists had imagined, demanding a diversion of resources that might otherwise go to assuring a male's long term-health."

Finding a Spiritual Teacher

A passage in my previous book, *The Complete Empath Toolkit* described the experience of meeting my spiritual teacher, Bro, a shaman from Canada who traveled three or four times a year to Santa Fe to work with his 10 students who resided there.

> *He had his eye on me. I knew it, and there was nothing else I could do. I walked around camp pretending not to notice or be affected by his stares. He stalked my every move. He was called simply "Bro." And yet he was not just any spiritual elder. He was "The" Bro, intimidating beyond belief. His reputation preceded him wherever he went. We were regaled with story after legendary story. The Canadian government once hired him to run sweat lodge ceremonies to heal their hard-core inmates – serial killers and rapists. The rumor around camp was that he got nearly 500 inmates paroled through his healing ability. He was subtle, drawing only the proper amount of attention to himself. When he was in a good mood, after morning coffee, he had a hearty, gregarious, and infectious laugh. He had a special penchant for making fun of people, for tearing down the ego, and sometimes for purposeful humiliation. In short, he was a paradox. He was called a "heyoka," otherwise known in Native circles as a sacred clown.*

While it's not necessary to find a drill sergeant shaman like I did, it is essential that you find someone who you can trust, someone who will lend you their ear, and someone who can *witness* you. Simply being witnessed is a powerful, but under-appreciated, healing method. This occurs when it is pointed out to you the times that you are functioning optimally and the times when you are getting in your way. This witnessing is often all that is required to propel you forward.

There are many spiritual teachers who have established internationally known schools of healing. If this way of learning is not an option for you, ask the universe to send you a teacher, a mentor, a counselor, a shaman, or a healer who will work with you one-on-one, and possibly, just possibly, a mentor who will be compassionate enough to wipe your nose for you when it's too filled with mucous from your endless tears, like mine did for me.

One good recommendation is shaman Dr. Alberto Villoldo's Four Winds Society. The school offers master's degree programs in shamanism and energy medicine. Dr. Villoldo has written about shamanism and healing over his 30 year career, and any of his books or DVDs would be an excellent introduction to the requirements for full-fledged healers. Barbara Brennan is a renowned energy healer who wrote *Hands of Light: A Guide to Healing Through the Human Energy Field*. She established the Barbara Brennan School of Healing in the United States, Europe, and Japan. She has written extensively about chakras, which we will now explore.

Learning About Your Chakras

Chakras are powerful energy centers that are the basis of how we experience the world. Chakra means "Wheel of Light" in Sanskrit. Barbara Brennan describes the body's 7 primary chakras. These spinning energy centers extend from the front and back of a person's body and vibrate so fast, like the blades of a fan, that we can't see them. And yet, any intuitive or sensitive person can tell you that they are there, serving the body for our highest good.

Years of energetic abuse or taking in negativity from other persons leads to over-stimulation of the heart and the solar plexus chakras. My clients often talk about how their chakras are blocked. They experience these blocks through physical sensations such as tension in the heart and pulsing or throbbing of the solar plexus. There is often a pattern of shifting back and forth between excess energy or lack of energy. Some clients simply describe these sensations as being blocked or feeling hurt in some way. Others are more descriptive and state their physical sensations with more precision. I ask clients to make contact with their chakras with precision. (See the dialogue exercise below.)

Chakras close down to protect you from feeling the lower vibratory energy that emanates from other people—anger, fear, hurt, grief, sadness, and loneliness. This is a natural protection mechanism that is initially helpful.

Regardless of your level of sensitivity, you do have the ability to perceive and soak up the emotions of the person standing in line in front of you at Subway. Think about how many of these public interactions you have as you move through your day. Then take that and multiply it by the number of days you've been alive. You can see that your nervous system may be overtaxed because of your sensitivity. Over time, your chakras begin to shut down due to stress.

This shutting down can develop into habits that are maladaptive. We may withdraw from social situations, preferring to remain by ourselves in the relative comfort of our own energy. This leads to a Catch-22, because we are social creatures who are meant to exchange energy.

Metaphysical Associations of the Chakras

Root Chakra (Beneath your perineum)
> Element: Earth
> Qualities: Being grounded in one's power. Patience. Structure.
Stability. Security. Being able to manifest your dreams.
> Positive Archetype: Mother
> Negative Archetype: Victim

2nd Chakra (Reproductive area)
> Element: Water
> Qualities: Unrestricted sexuality and free-flowing emotion.
Ability to receive pleasure and abundance.
> Positive Archetype: Emperor/Empress
> Negative Archetype: Martyr

3rd Chakra (Solar Plexus)
> Element: Fire
> Qualities: Leadership. Passion. Instinctual knowledge. Gut
feelings. Confidence (or the opposite, fear). Self-worth. Self-esteem.

Personal power.
>   Positive Archetype: Warrior
>   Negative Archetype: Servant

4th Chakra (Heart Center)
>   Element: Air
>   Qualities: Unity. Brother/sisterhood. Love. Peace. Forgiveness.
Empathy. To give and receive love are the life issues associated with this
chakra.
>   Positive Archetype: Lover
>   Negative Archetype: Actor/Actress

5th Chakra (Throat Center)
>   Element: Ether/Space
>   Qualities: Communication. Creativity. Truthfulness. Integrity
(Also the center where grief gets lodged). Harnessing your will and
expressing your true self are the life issues associated with this chakra.
>   Positive Archetype: Communicator
>   Negative Archetype: Silent Child

6th Chakra (Brow or Third Eye Center)
>   Element: Ether/Space
>   Qualities: Mindful knowing. Fully developed intuition in the
form of visionary experiences. Wisdom and discernment. Imagination.
Knowing and being able to apply knowledge for everyone's highest good
is the life issue of this chakra.
>   Positive Archetype: Wise Elder
>   Negative Archetype: Intellectual Academic

7th Chakra (Crown Center)
>   Element: The Entire Cosmos
>   Qualities: Spiritual transcendence. Understanding. Grace.
Serenity. Oneness with All that Is. Connection with the entire Medicine
Circle and Hoop of Life.
>   Positive Archetype: Guru

Negative Archetype: Egoist

One way we can take responsibility for ourselves is by working mentally and physically with our chakras. Give them our attention. I teach a process that will help you dialogue with your chakras. Talk to them and ask them to stop always protecting you. Pat them down; give them a rub. Treat them with TLC, and they will remain open. At various points throughout the day, physically rub your chakras. Then put essential oils on them or perhaps rub salt into them. Most of all, ask for healing light energy to come to them. They will open automatically in response to your request for assistance.

Exercise: Dialoguing with your Chakras

1. Drop your awareness from you head to your heart.
2. Rest there. Notice which chakra needs attention.
3. Place your awareness in the front of that chakra. Notice the quality of energy.
4. Place your awareness in the back of that chakra. Notice the quality of energy.
5. Make thought contact with the chakra. Thank it for its help and protection all these years. Tell the chakra that habitual closing is no longer needed. Ask the chakra to remain open and visualize the chakra being open in your mind's eye.
6. What color energy is the chakra? Ignore anything you know about the colors associated with each chakra. *However you perceive the color of your chakra is valid for you.*
7. Ask the chakra what color energy it wants or needs to support it. Ask the universe for that frequency of energy to be sent to the chakra. Notice what this does to your chakra. Spend a few minutes running this color energy.
8. Thank the chakra. Close this exercise by asking for it to send you messages throughout your day. Tell your chakra that you want to continue the dialogue and that you are ready to listen to its message.

Becoming a Spiritual Detective: Watching and Listening For Clues

Navigating the new age involves learning to ask the right questions and becoming a spiritual detective. Yes, you are the Sherlock Holmes of the new age! Get out your hats and metaphorical magnifying glasses because that's what's being asked of you—or more accurately, it's what you are asking of yourself.

Learning Who You Are is like placing one hand in front of the other and traveling down the rope of consciousness. Do you get a vague idea that your true work may involve working with kids? OK, tap into that feeling. Now, turn up the volume on that feeling and follow the energy to where it leads, whether that be more feelings, images, and dreams.

We detectives follow the clues, look at the puzzle pieces, and ask for more information. We sink deeper and deeper into our experiences, our visions, our premonitions, and our intuitions because there is *always* more information to be gained if only we ask.

Spiritual Detectives Are OPEN

In our everyday lives as spiritual detectives, we operate by using four primary principles summarized by the acronym OPEN. OPEN stands for Observing, Perceiving, Experiencing, and Noticing. Each of these words refers to the process of engaging and refining the 6-sensory experience. Each word, whether it be "noticing" or "experiencing," relates to what is happening with our sensory input at any given time.

As I guide clients in becoming a spiritual detective, I ask, "What are you noticing right now?" Whether I am leading them through chakra clearing exercises, or whether we are calling in the energies of their spiritual guides, my questions are always the same: "What are you observing?" "What are you experiencing?" "What are you perceiving?" "What are you noticing?" In this way, clients learn to pay attention to sensory input that may otherwise be ignored. Paying attention almost always involves using one of the four words represented by OPEN.

Here's an example of being a spiritual detective. During coaching sessions, I engage my clients in becoming aware of the quality of energy in their bodies. Perhaps a client reports sensory distress or energy blockage in the heart area. To dislodge this energy in the heart, we ask for an amplification of the feeling of that we want, instead of the feeling we don't want. Usually the client will ask to create a feeling of peace, calmness, or tranquility.

Because everything is connected, creating this type of energy leads to changes and improvements in other areas of the body. To help my clients become spiritual detectives, I will simply ask them to follow the "energy rope" with their consciousness wherever it leads in the body. It may involves noticing a tingle in the kidney region. It may involve a feeling of energy being amplified down the leg. Perhaps it involves a sensation of the third eye being opened. The point is that we must be Observant, Perceptive, Experiencing, and Noticing in order to realize that there is usually a higher message behind the energy changes.

If you notice during energy work that your kidneys are being triggered (which is often mistaken for lower back pain), what would that allow you to do? Perhaps you would get a special tea for kidney support. Perhaps you would make a doctor's appointment to get your kidney function tested. Or perhaps you would schedule some bodywork for the kidney area. Each of these options would lead to improved health and better energy flow in your body. You wouldn't have noticed that your kidneys were asking for support unless you were OPEN.

The same refined consciousness that allows you to be aware of the energy in your kidneys will allow you to become aware of other dimensions and spiritual planes. By training yourself to become aware of your body's energy, you can also train yourself to become more conscious of the higher spiritual realms—especially the messages that your Highest Self has for you.

To put the OPEN process into action, I've found a helpful metaphor for viewing ourselves: we are like satellite dishes. And just like satellite dishes, we broadcast output and receive input at the same time. We've got a big dish on our heads, broadcasting to the world day and night! According to Dr. Jose Arguelles, Mayan science was based on principles of resonance, sounding and reverberating. To the Mayans, reality is frequency, in which "vibrational signals pass from a transmitter to a receiver." Just like a satellite dish, we must make sense of, or otherwise perceive, a signal. And one of the major ways in which we can do this is by using our three brains.

Embracing Our Three Brains

Scientists who study MRI's say that we use only 10 percent of our brain power. Perhaps it might be more accurate to say that we use only a small fraction of our energetic resources. The brain is an important processing center for energetic data, but there are two other important resource centers as well: the gut and the heart chakra.

Western medicine ignores the "brains" of the gut and the heart, much to our detriment. The gut area is the home of the enteric nervous system, an area that has actually contains more nerves than the brain itself. There are about 100,000,000 neurons in the small intestine alone, which is more than in the spinal column. Messages moving upward from the gut to the brain outnumber messages moving down from the brain to the gut by 9 to 1! The enteric nervous system, which includes the large intestine, the anus, the stomach, and the umbilicus (belly button), is the body's truth detector. It takes our experiences, eliminates clutter, and leaves the remaining data for our benefit.

> Phrases that reflect the power of the gut include:
> *"That was a gutsy thing to do"*
> *"He's gutless"*
> *"I had a gut feeling it wasn't right."*
> *"My gut instinct is to say..."*
> *"I hate his guts."*
> *"He spilled his guts."*

The heart chakra, at the center of our chakra system, is also a type of brain. In the heart chakra, the upper chakras (throat, third eye, and crown) and the lower chakras (anything below the heart) meet. The function of the heart chakra is to take data from above and below and make sense of it.

The heart chakra gives output through feelings and emotions. In my coaching practice, we acknowledge the heart as a brain. It gives us feelings, emotions, and memories to sort through. We follow that data, digging deep like a good detective, asking the heart chakra additional questions and receiving answers.

The language of spirit comes in blips, bleeps, vague sensations, tingles, feelings, things we can't explain. I wish I had a dime for every time I've heard, "I can't put words to it." Precisely! The ego (small mind) and the Highest Self (the part of you which is God) speak two different languages! Learning to navigate your way through our new era involves learning and mastering a new language. You can forget Rosetta Stone! This language involves communicating directly and clearly with your Highest Self.

Each of us perceives energy and data from spiritual sources in different ways. In the new age one of your primary tasks is to identify how Spirit attempts to communicate with you. Is it primarily through symbols, feelings, or another way? Another important task is to tell your spirit guides what certain symbols mean to you so that they you can communicate with you accurately.

Floor to Ceiling Exercise:

Lie on your back, flat on the floor, with your head tilted backwards. Then look up at the ceiling. Now with your intention framed on a new field of vision, pretend the floor is the ceiling and the ceiling is the floor.

This exercise may not only make you laugh, especially if you do it with another person, but it helps you to see things that you have not noticed, such as what the ceiling looks like from the floor's perspective. This exercise is analogous to what it's like being in the dream world, astral traveling, where everything literally is upside down! The ordinary rules of what we think are reality don't apply! Make this a regular practice. You engage new neural pathways in the brain when you do this.

The act of looking at the room differently will allow you more power and perception to see your *life* differently.

Creating Your Own Rosetta Stone: Learning Your Spiritual Alphabet

In much the same way as the previous exercise activates new neural pathways, here's another exercise to help you see things differently and learn the language of Spirit: What is the color of the number 1? What about the number 2? Number 3? Go through each of the numbers 1-10 and you may be surprised to learn that each number can be perceived as having color energy.

The next time you perceive the number 2, you may associate it with the color red. Being the good spiritual detective that you are, you will take that deeper and ask for more information. You can ask, What does that mean? You may associate red with fire, passion, or love. Or perhaps, like me, you associate it with blood. Whatever it is, decide what a certain color means in general terms so that the next time you see the color in your dreams or your consciousness, you will understand what spirit is trying to tell you. Blue is often associated with coolness or ice. So when you perceive this color, it may mean that spirit is showing you important information about needing to cool down your body or your mind. Or perhaps, for you, blue will become associated with grief, depression, or sad feelings. It is up to you do decide what a particular symbol means for you, and going through the color alphabet is a good way to start.

Here are some common archetypal symbols on which you can meditate:

Symbol	Common Meanings
Rabbits	fertility
Bears	protection, nurturance
Cars	movement from point A to point B
Eagle	vision

Crabs   protection
Elevators   consciousness moving from heaven down to Earth and vice versa.

Recently, Spirit told me that a dear client would benefit from hypnotherapy. Vera is a delightful Russian woman, age 42, full of vibrancy, empathy, and intuitive power. She is fully engaged in discovering her intuitive gifts. She is learning that she has a karmic role to play in transmuting darkness into Light. I received an email from Vera in which she shared a story of how Spirit is teaching her about her own medicine. Through describing a shamanic journey experience, she illustrates how to engage Spirit and ask for more information:

"I felt a strong pressure on both sides of my head and a very warm energy— almost heat there—and it felt as if it was 'rewiring' the brain. It felt like a Lilac tent, and being there just felt so good. ...so I started asking: Who is my power animal? Suddenly a word distinctly came to my mind—'Mohawk.' I didn't know what it meant. So I thought: 'I don't know this English word ...please give me the animal's name in Russian or show me a picture,' and again a strong short word comes to my mind: 'Mohawk.' It was funny. When we were sharing the experience, I asked the leader what kind of animal Mohawk is and they said that one Indian tribe is called Mohawk. And then I learned that the owner of the store is having Mohawk Elder Leonard Fourhawks give intuitive readings this Saturday for her 5th year store celebration! So I decided to sign up for a reading—going there tomorrow morning. Maybe I'll learn something!"

This is an example of how Spirit is constantly guiding us. The key is that we have to ask, just like Vera did. She was a spiritual detective, receiving guidance and taking it deeper by asking additional questions based on the information that she received. In these new times, we never stop engaging our inner detective!

Another client, James, has been becoming more in touch with messages from his Highest Self. He has an affinity for listening to the message of Spirit through numerology and numbers. A week after an especially profound coaching session, he sent me an email in which he described how Spirit is constantly "dropping clues" as to where our true identity lies.

"On my way home Wednesday evening, I decided to stop at the grocery store. As I turned the corner, in the direction of the store, my first angelic moment! I saw a license plate that read: 'CO Lisc #_ _ _ 111'

I parked the car, went into the grocery store and returned to the car. I turned around to back out of the parking space, and OMG!! There was a CO License Plate # 333-TGS. The company I work for is the The Gourmet Spoon!

Then, as I drove out of the grocery parking lot onto the street, another CO Lisc # 111 _ _ was directly in front of me, parked on the street.

I pulled out my 'handy dandy' angelic numerology guide and read the messages.

111: 'Monitor your thoughts carefully and be sure to only think about what you choose... not what you don't want! This is a sign that there is a gate of opportunity opening up.'

333: 'The Ascended Masters are near you, desiring you to know that you have the help, love, and companionship that you need.'

Another moment of Joy, on this journey ...'we' are not alone! This happens all the time!

'Now', I have to 'Trust' it...
'Now', I have to 'Accept' it ...
'Now', it's time to 'Soar' with it. "

James and I had spent several sessions talking about moving past his fear by taking actions in alignment with his highest intention. A week after sending me this email, James packed his bags and, in a leap of faith, moved away from Denver, Colorado, where he had spent several miserable years. There is a saying: "Leap and the net will appear." James took this guidance to heart and is now living in Wisconsin where he is thriving.

And then there's the story of Kiko, an 82-year-old woman looking for adventure! She left her house in Salt Lake City, Utah, and traveled 1,000 miles to join our spiritual community for a powerful 8-day vision quest ceremony. To coincide with this ceremony, she had sold many of her old possessions in preparation for a new "birth." I was awestruck at the amount of faith this woman demonstrated. She hauled rocks as we rebuilt our fire pit and she helped us to stabilize the trees as we rebuilt the sweat lodge. Kiko is an example of full-throttle spiritual living. She shows us that no matter how old you think you are, there is always room for adventure and learning. The last I heard, Kiko was back in Salt Lake, armed with new experiences, and enjoying an expanded circle of friends and family.

The Language Cop: NBW

Letters formed together are nothing more than pieces, like a jigsaw puzzle, formed in certain combinations to represent an energetic state. The word happiness is: H+A+P+P+I+N+E+S+S. In other words, it is the energy of H plus the energy of A plus the energy of P, and so on. It's a formula; a recipe, if you will, intended to produce an energetic state in the person who is perceiving.

Thus, the alphabet is a little bit like baking. In cooking, a little bit of salt, with some milk, cream, vanilla, and eggs, when put together in a bowl, produces vanilla pudding. Language structures our reality in the same way. Therefore, we must be careful to use a good recipe, to choose our symbols carefully and deliberately, so that we get in the right flow and have a good tasting experience!

Words are a representation of what we call forth into our reality. They structure our reality. Every utterance from our mouth is a prayer. Therefore, we must choose what we ask for *carefully*. You can literally re-write your life story to include more of what you want.

Psychokinesis is not some fancy or magic talent that only a few have. We all have this talent and use it every day. The only difference between those who can move mountains with their minds and those who can't is the quickness with which we can manifest. We manifest everything we think, some quicker than others (thankfully!). So if you have a negative thought, it *will* hurt you. In the same breath, a positive thought *will* help you, immensely.

One day I had the brilliant idea to do energy work on my television. I went to the TV, placed my hands just above it, and started to run energy. Later that day, when I attempted to turn the television on, a quick burst of flames shot from the back of the television. That was the end of that experiment and the beginning of a new cautiousness in how I applied my thoughts and my energy. Seeing the flames was enough evidence to convince me that I *was* powerful, I don't need to do anything to prove it, and I had better be very cautious and careful as to what I wanted to call into my reality.

The same principle applies for every word that comes out of our mouths. "The Language Cop" is a device for us to remember to be careful with our utterances, and to eliminate the use of three words entirely. These are words came from the old paradigm in which we perceived fear and lack. In our new era, these words can be replaced.

The acronym NBW stands for the three words: *Need*, *But*, and *Why*. It also stands for "*No Banned Words.*" This may help you remember to eliminate the use of three words that begin with NBW entirely from your vocabulary.

<u>*Need:*</u>   You don't need anything. If you believe you need something, you give your power away. You already have everything you need. Spirit makes sure of that. Sometimes we believe we need protection. While this might be true at times, the word "need" only feeds into what can become an over-generalized and illusory creation of our reality. The word "need" can be replaced with the word "want" in almost all cases. Consider the difference between, "I need to do this...." versus "I want do this....."   Need implies that there is some outside force looking over us, demanding that we get in line. The use of the word "want" acknowledges the truth that it is ourselves who hold the power over the creation of our reality.

<u>*But:*</u> The word "but" is probably the most useless word in the English language. In every instance it can be replaced with the word

"and." The word "but" *cuts off energy.* It also puts people on the defensive. When the human ego hears a phrase followed by the word "but," it immediately gets suspicious and goes on the defensive. No doubt you've experienced this phenomenon yourself. "I really like you, but..." revokes whatever affirmative statement you said prior to it. It's a negative word with limited effectiveness. You can replace the word "but" with "and" and you will be saying the same thing. The beauty of using "and" instead of "but" is that it allows for *multiple realities at the same time!* The word "and" allows for energy flow.

Consider the following exchange:

"I really like you, **but**....I can't date you right now because of other commitments."

"I really like you, **and** I can't date you right now because of other commitments."

Which exchange feels better to you? I have a hunch that the latter may be more acceptable for your ego. Replacing "but" with "and" eliminates defensiveness and promotes better harmony in your relationships with everyone—lovers, friends, children. Try it, and perhaps you'll be pleasantly surprised how deeply you'll connect with others.

Why: I often hear phrases from clients such as "Why am I so sensitive?" "Why do I feel so wounded?" and "Why do I suffer so much?" I encourage my clients to eliminate "why questions" because they are stagnant. "Why questions" don't lead to worthwhile information nor do they lead to productive action. Even if you get an answer to your why question (such as having your sensitivity originate from an unresolved karmic issue in a past life), where does that leave you? Stuck in your head, and that's it.

So, instead of asking "why questions," I recommend that you begin all of your questions with the word "How?" I remind clients that what they are really saying when they ask "Why do I suffer so much?" is actually "How can I cope with my life so that I don't suffer so much?" Do you notice the difference? It's a radical paradigm shift. "How" questions lead to productive action. "Why" questions can sometimes contain the energy of protest.

Find a Practice Partner

In my online classes, I encourage participants to pair up with another participant to do intuitive readings with each other. I suggest this for you as well. You might say, "But there isn't anyone I trust." The act of practicing will actually create trust. The point of having a practice partner is to learn to build confidence in your psychic abilities and trust that what you perceive is accurate.

Practicing with a partner will amplify your learning your spiritual alphabet because intuiting a vision of something can mean many things. It could be literal or symbolic. Take for instance, a bear. A bear could be masculine or scary for one person and soft, feminine, and a symbol of guardianship or protection for another. In the future, if Spirit shows you a bear, what will that symbol mean for you?

It is important to not get caught up in the literal details of practice intuitive readings. Rather, see what you are given as broad symbols with many possible interpretations. If you see your psychic practice partner riding on a gigantic ocean ship, how will you interpret that? That question can only be answered through trial and error practice, in which you discern for yourself what the symbols mean. Sometimes the visions I receive are detailed and relate to an experience in a client's life. At other times the vision I receive is a symbolic message. With practice, you will understand the difference. Take the leap. Ask someone you know if they would be willing to trade psychic readings with you. If you don't know anyone, ask the universe to send you someone. It will happen. It's only a matter of time.

Start a Psychic Diary

As you learn about your spiritual alphabet and how Spirit communicates with you, it is useful to have a dedicated psychic notebook and/or dream journal. In this notebook you will write down random psychic messages and intuitions as you move through your day. This notebook will reflect your unique soul, so choose a nice notebook.

If you're the artistic type, make it visually appealing to you. I go through a notebook every few months. I use hardbound notebooks so I can place them on my library shelves and use them as reference books. It's fun to go back and see what random messages eventually come true over time.

Remembering Dreams

Messages contained in the dreamworld help you decode and demystify the language of Spirit and help you make sense of the energy and messages you experience in waking life. This is a language that speaks in energy, symbols, and feelings. Just like learning a foreign language, it takes time and effort to perfect.

The biggest obstacle to mastering the language of dreams is an inability to remember dreams. What most people don't realize is that dream recall is a learned skill, and an inability to remember does not mean there is anything wrong with the way your brain works. It just takes a little bit of sustained effort and a few nighttime behavioral changes. So, do you want to heighten your dream awareness? The answer that I hear consistently from my inner power coaching clients is a strong yes!

If that is the case for you, then it may be helpful to realize that Dream Wisdom is something that comes directly proportional to a) the strength of your intention and b) the strength of your actions. If you already are able to remember your dreams, give yourself a pat on the back! Only about 3 to 10 percent of individuals regularly remember their dreams. For the rest of us, it's a skill that takes perseverance and hard work. Your dream "muscle" becomes stronger with intention and especially with action.

Every night we have an opportunity to connect with our Highest Selves, our guides, and our guardians. In order to connect with those sources of information, we need to make an effort and show Spirit that we mean business! Over the last 15 years of dream study, I've discovered some effective and simple techniques for helping cultivate dream wisdom. You may want to try some or all of these suggestions.

Here are some concrete action steps that will help you on your quest:

1. Just before sleep, actually voice your intention to remember dreams. While you may initially resist the suggestion to physically voice the words, I have found that it is more helpful than simply saying it mentally. There is something about engaging the vocal cords that helps to energetically program your nervous system to carry out your wishes.

2. Create a dream altar on a table near your bed. On the dream altar, place a dream notebook, several pens, and a flashlight or other lighting source. I have found that placing a quartz crystal on the altar raises the vibration and helps you tune in to the dream frequency.

3. Date your dream journal entry before you fall asleep each night, as this will help produce an expectation to remember.

4. If you do not mind the intrusion into your sleep, you may want to set your alarm clock to wake you at a specified point during the night. If you are worried about waking a partner, drinking several large glasses of water prior to bed may be another way to assure you will wake up (and help you to remember).

5. Establish regular sleep routines. This means starting your sleep in the same position every night, as well as going to bed and waking at the same time. Do not eat heavy meals before bed as this will interfere with your sleep cycle.

6. Upon waking, gently probe your mind. Pay attention to bodily sensations. If you don't immediately remember, stay with a feeling and follow it deeper by asking the feeling to be amplified. Specific recollections will often be triggered by focusing on vague feelings and sensations. If you're in a different physical position than you were while dreaming, try shifting your body back into that position. This will often be enough to trigger recall. If you cannot remember an image or event,

stay with even the smallest feeling, try to make it larger, and it often will trigger a memory.

7. When you write down your dreams, include the sensory impressions that come to mind: colors, images, sounds, tastes, people's expressions, settings, feelings, and emotions.

8. If you do remember a dream, especially if it's in detail, make sure to write as much as you can. If you're sleepy or feeling lazy while awaking (common), then use your willpower to bust through that. Even though you are groggy and tired when waking, it's worth it to write as much as you can before you forget. Here's text, verbatim, from one of my more amazing, and yet frustrating, dream journal entries. It sounded like I had a near death experience. I wrote the following: *"I actually died. I drifted away. Things were then neutral and then sped up very fast into a vortex of life recall. Every memory of my life happened very fast. I was in awe."* My current reaction to reading this entry is "That's it?" Probably one of the most amazing dream state experiences I have had, and I didn't write more? This vague entry highlights the importance of taking those few extra seconds while sleepy to be as specific and detailed as possible when writing down our dreams.

9. Some persons have reported that certain dietary supplements (for example, lecithin, melatonin) may promote memory and dream recall. Please consult with your health care provider before starting any supplement or diet program.

10. Check out the Association for the Study of Dreams. (www.ASDreams.org). It is the best source on the web for a societal and scientific focus on dreaming. I joined ASD in 1996 and have attended past conferences, which are exceptionally fun!

Symbols: The Language of Dreams

Decoding the language of dreams involves decoding the language of symbols. Just as you use symbols to communicate with the spirit realm, the spirit realm gives you symbols every night that you must decode.

Simple dream dictionaries you can get for a few bucks in the checkout lines of the grocery store are acceptable for the average person who has only a passing spiritual interest. For the advanced student, however, you may likely want to investigate the symbols and the actions of your dreams with precision and come to your own conclusions about what they mean.

In dream interpretation, symbols are the most important way to discover the message of the dream. The other important elements of good dream decoding are feelings, actions, and how you react in the dream. If you are angry and go off on someone in a rage, then Spirit may be asking you to learn to control your rage. Spirit always gives us "lessons" in the nightly dream school until we get it right. If we constantly are running away from someone or something in our dreams, this is a pretty good indicator that in our own lives, we tend to escape from pain or responsibilities by avoidance. Spirit may be asking you to *face* your responsibilities instead.

Technique: Dream Re-Entry

In meditation upon waking from a dream, close your eyes and go back into the dream with your imagination. Using the above example, you could create a different, more productive course of action instead of running away. You could confront whatever is chasing you and voice your lack of fear. You can point a finger and shoot waves of Light at whatever is persecuting you. You could engage it in dialogue and ask it what it needs. The possibilities are endless. If you practice this with every disturbing dream, your earthly reality will begin to mirror the re-created dream. Giving your dreams different endings trains your nervous system so that the next time someone chases you in the dreamworld, you can make different decisions. With sustained practice, your days of running away from perceived threats will be over.

Chapter Four

Empaths and Highly Sensitive People: Why Now?

In 1998 I had my first reading with a psychic practitioner. I was living behind a Chinese restaurant that constantly smelled of egg drop soup on the corner of 12th and Wilshire in Santa Monica, California. I was a recent transplant from the Midwest, where I was raised, and had come to California in search of mysticism and adventure. After seeing an advertisement for cheap ($15) psychic readings with students of the Clearsight Psychic Institute, I took a risk and made an appointment.

The psychic and I settled into our chairs, facing each other, and got comfortable. Or, more accurately, she got comfortable. I was terrified. I think her name was Judy. Her first act was to push the "Record" button on the tape recorder.

"I'm going to read your aura," she announced.

I braced myself for the worst. Being seen by others was not a strong suit for me.

"Oh, my," she said. "I've never quite seen anything like it. You have no boundaries. Your aura is completely translucent."

Her direct manner of speaking, combined with my insecurity and triple-Scorpio energetic makeup, created an explosive mix that triggered my worst habitual defenses. I got up, shouted a few things about learning how to work with people, and stormed out of the room without paying my $15.

Several years later, I sent the school a check for teaching me an important lesson about myself.

~~~~

Over the last decade, there has been a growing awareness that many individuals on the planet are extraordinarily sensitive to energy.

This energy can take many forms, such as perceiving the emotions of others, sensing the desires of animals, and being in tune with the Earth and the environment. What I know, and what many of you know, is that you are more sensitive than others. You probably have known this since you were a child, when you could just look at someone and "know" their intentions or their emotions.

Interest in this subject has been exploding, compounding itself on a daily basis. Here's a recent email:

"The biggest problem I'm having and not knowing how to deal with is the energy I sense. I can't see a person's aura. But I feel it. I feel the energy people give. This caused so many problems with my family growing up. Often there was a lot of stress and tension in the house. Negative energy affected me to the point I was incredibly stressed. I would try to help but no one would listen, so I became angry and pretty much was never there. I feel my friends' emotions to the point they almost become my own. All the while fighting all of it and getting angry that I can't stop. I'm tired. Maybe I need medication. I tried that too, for almost three years. It made me numb I suppose. I got off it a few months ago. Maybe I do need to be on it. I feel crazy enough. Lol."

Chances are that if you are an empath, you will see yourself in the above message. I keep a special folder in my email program where I put these messages. It's not possible for me to respond to each one, but I read them all. When I read messages from empaths who share their stories, I am struck by how similar our experiences are. We use the same words, have similar coping mechanisms, and discount ourselves because we are so gifted in seeing, experiencing, and affirming others!

Why now? Why this explosion of interest in empaths? The fact that many of us are identifying ourselves as empaths, or highly sensitive, is likely a reflection of reunification, of mending the circle. It reflects the acceleration of consciousness, of dropping false "truths" of the ego. Individuals who have lived their lives in defeated isolation, thinking that their sensitivity made them different or crazy are now able to see themselves positively with the affirming terms highly sensitive person or empath.

Jerome Kagen, a Harvard psychologist, is one of the pioneers in studying highly sensitive people. To him, sensitivity is an observable trait. In the 1970's he studied shyness in children and found that body levels of certain stress hormones were much higher in sensitive children than in those who were not. This is because sensitive people are in a constant state of alertness and hyper-arousal. He also found that sensitive children had more activity in the right hemispheres of their brains. This is not surprising since the right side is associated with creativity, non-linearity, and spiritual and transpersonal experiences. He also found that about 20 percent of his study participants were what he called "highly reactive," that is, deeply sensitive to external stimuli.

Psychologist Dr. Elaine Aron was the first to write about highly sensitive people by using that term. In 1996 she published *The Highly Sensitive Person.* A benefit of her work is that she uses psychological terms that are accessible to the average reader. Through her scientific research, she has helped normalize a trait, sensitivity, that was previously not appreciated. She explored the subject using the language of the human nervous system and physical body. Her basic premise? Sensitivity to external stimulation in all forms is a consistently-found human trait that has advantages. "Like the fire department, we HSPs mostly respond to false alarms," she writes. "But if our sensitivity saves a life even once, it is a trait that has a genetic payoff. When our trait leads to arousal, it is a nuisance. But it is a part of a package deal with many advantages." Aron's research (telephone samples of 300 randomly selected adults) confirmed Kagen's finding that 20 percent of adults can be classified as "extremely" or "quite a bit" sensitive. She does not explore the spiritual ramifications of high sensitivity, however, which many authors, including myself, are striving to do.

That's where other authors such as David Ritchey enter the picture. He is an example of the new breed of researchers who explore the esoteric spiritual realms while at the same time being respectful of science and research. Ritchey has researched what he calls "the anomalously sensitive person" and has written a groundbreaking book,

The HISS of the ASP: Understanding the Anomalously Sensitive Person. One of the benefits of his research is that he is open to transpersonal experiences. He goes beyond the work of Dr. Aron to explore UFO's and paranormal experiences.

Physician Dr. Judith Orloff is a pioneer who has studied empaths. Her New York Times best-selling books have popularized the term "intuitive empath," most notably in *Second Sight* in which she described her life journey. Many empaths have first discovered the term through her books.

Rose Rosetree's book *Empowered by Empathy: 25 ways to Fly in Spirit* explores skills and theory. She talks about her personal experiences and those of her clients with humor and lightheartedness. "Skilled empathy helps people live with a deeper spiritual awareness," she says. She has coined the term "malled": the feeling sensitive people get when they enter crowded malls and are bombarded with stimuli.

What term do we use to make sense of our experiences? Empaths or highly sensitive people? Which label applies, and to whom? There is a difference between highly sensitive people and empaths, according to Rose Rosetree. She writes, "Not all HSPs are empaths but, so far, I have yet to find an empath who isn't a sensitive."

Empaths are a special *sub-class* of highly sensitive people. While I have yet to publish scientific research on the topic, it is my observation that empaths account for roughly one fourth of all highly sensitive people. By extrapolation, empaths are roughly five percent of the total population. Since you are reading this book, you may likely identify more readily with empath because it includes a spiritual sensitivity that the term "highly sensitive people" doesn't quite capture.

For this reason, I will focus on empaths, whose sensitivity is connected to something larger than themselves. While a highly sensitive person might chalk up his or her traits to genetics or psychology, empaths tend to see their traits and gifts as coming from a higher spiritual order. Highly sensitive people may live very fulfilling lives but not necessarily look at the spiritual or larger societal implications of their abilities.

On the other hand, empaths take the trait of being highly sensitive into realms of social responsibility and a *mission* to help other people. We tend to understand our suffering as burdens that are borne because God has asked us to carry such burdens for our fellow man.

We may not fully understand why, but we understand enough to know that we have a responsibility to ourselves and others to live in integrity. Because we link personal sensitivity with psychic and mystical realms, we tend to be exceptionally responsible about our personal healing. We understand that there are spiritual ramifications for our suffering, and that we must keep ourselves as clean and clear as possible so that we may be *channels of healing* for other people.

You cannot change the fact that you are an empath. You either are or you aren't. It is not teachable. It's not something you can learn.

Here are some of the primary traits of empaths:

Empaths are exceptionally sensitive to emotions and needs of others.

Empaths tend to be good listeners.

Empaths often put others' needs before their own.

Empaths generally do not understand cruelty or violence and would never harm another person or living being.

Empaths feel things deeply as they happen and will often have visceral reactions to scenes on television or in the movies.

Empaths tend to be deeply in touch with emotions, and some cry easily.

Empaths can become overstimulated easily and are sensitive to chaos.

Empaths tend to withdraw as a coping mechanism to stress.

Many empaths are clairsentient, the psychic experience of "knowing," and are deeply in touch with psychic and spiritual realms. Many have an interest in or experiences with the paranormal.

Being an empath means that you are always "on" to process other people's feelings and energy. You have a gift, or in many cases, what may feel like a curse! Being an empath can indeed be challenging. You feel *everything*, even if you are not aware of it. Many empaths become blocked in their heart areas. They feel tension and constriction there because the heart area is overtaxed with repeated exposure to negative stimuli and unpleasant emotions.

Many of us shut down overwhelming feelings through mood-altering substances. We disengage from experiences because constantly perceiving others' negative experiences can be painful. Many addicts are unconscious empaths who have never experienced the dignity of knowing that they are gifted. Instead, they believe themselves to be damaged or wrong. Nothing could be further from the truth.

Being what some call "hypersensitive" to the feelings of others is *not a bad thing*. It does *not* mean you are co-dependent. There is *nothing wrong with you,* although it may sometimes feel that way. Because your energetic boundaries are diffuse, you can feel, and in many cases, take on, the pain of others.

While this can be helpful to others, it can leave you severely drained, feeling like you're running on empty. As you awaken to your empathic gifts, and if you are to thrive, you must have the courage to plant your feet firmly on the ground and learn when to say *no*. Choose wisely. Just because you have this gift, you do not always need to use it.

With the gift of empathy comes responsibility. The primary responsibility is to become larger and to vibrate at a higher rate so that you are not overwhelmed by lower vibrations. Another responsibility is to be grounded. Learn to use the energy of the Earth energy so that the energies you perceive don't become stuck in your energy field or body. The techniques listed in Chapter 6 will help you to do this.

Becoming a conscious empath may give you relief, because you know that you are not alone, nor crazy. Despite what doctors may theorize, there is nothing wrong with you. Illnesses such as chronic fatigue, fibromyalgia, and even environmental sensitivities are often more likely attributable to outside influences than to anything about you.

It's not you. It really is not you.

As was discussed in Chapter 2, you are probably walking through life with the accumulated karma, emotions, and energy from other people. In addition to this, you are carrying the habits and memories of your ancestors. It would astound you to see the countless gun battles, murders, suicides, sicknesses, and bad habits that have been passed down to you through your DNA. These habits and memories are carried through generations, encoded in your genes, and are in the very cells of your body! *That means that you are not you.* You are your ancestors. And your ancestors are everyone and everything.

What if God asked many of us to incarnate on the Earth at this moment in time to help clean up the messes of the past? What if He asked some of us to carry the burdens of others so that we may help transmute the darkness? What if He asked some of us to be spiritual warriors, dutiful foot soldiers in the battle against the Shadow? And what if He asked us to become so deeply involved in this pursuit that we would volunteer to engage and heal the lower vibratory energy of other people?

I do believe that we can adapt and cope with our sensitivity, but we can't turn it off. Most of our misery comes from the frustration of banging our heads against the wall in an effort to be less sensitive. As Albert Einstein so famously said, the definition of insanity is doing the same thing over and over and expecting a different result.

So if we can't turn off our sensitivity, what can we do to cope?

The most important coping mechanism for empaths to learn is how to become grounded. In being grounded, the energy we accumulate will not affect us as much because it can more easily be discharged by the body in a conscious, mental manner (e.g. asking a tree to take lower-vibratory energy from us). And when we are grounded, the body is also able to more efficiently discharge energy through bodily processes such as coughing, trembling, sneezing, sweating, or urination.

By applying the exercises described in Chapter 6, you will amplify these processes with intention. You will learn how to connect to the Earth and ask the Earth to take energy you don't need from you. You will become cleaner, brighter, and more effective in your mission as an empath, whatever that means for you.

For more advanced exercises, see my eBook package, *The Complete Empath Toolkit*, on my website at EmpathConnection.com

Empath Awareness: What Reason Do I Have to Feel This Way?

If you are learning to adapt to your empathic gifts, or are just now becoming aware of yourself as an empath, the single most effective exercise is this one. As you go through your day, keep this question in the forefront of your awareness: *What reason do I have to feel this way?*

If you're an empath, there will very likely be no logical reason for you to feel the way you do. And if there is no reason, then what are the implications? You are probably experiencing the emotions, thoughts, or experiences of another person in your own body or mind. And if it's true that you feel others in your body, that you can hear their thoughts, that you are affected by their energies, what's the implication of that?

It means that by healing others, you heal yourself!

So if you are discovering that you may be an empath, then how do you handle that information? Learn as much as you can about being an empath. There are many internet forums where you can share with other empaths, including my Empath Connection facebook page. Meetup.com has empath groups in different areas of the country. Follow the instructions in this book. Get a spiritual mentor, discharge others' energy from your body through a physical exercise routine, get sober if you've got addiction, and most importantly, start accepting that you are made the way you are made for a reason.

Part of your spiritual path is discovering just what that reason is, for you. And it may very likely require you to begin a rigorous spiritual practice in which you begin to align your body, emotions, and mind. It can seem like a daunting task. You can take comfort in the fact that others have made the commitment to healing themselves, and are now thriving. And you can do the same thing.

Chapter Five

Mysteries Revealed: Experiences with the Paranormal

"People! Pay attention! Many multidimensional beings such as angels, Pleiadians, Sirians, Christ, and Mary Magdeline are moving in and out of your bodies! You are living in a time when they express themselves right within you. The point of seeing saucers and spaceships was to open you up, for you to realize that beings from other worlds are in your realm all around you. They are you, and you are being them unless you are a zombie. Remember, you created television to activate telepathy, telephones to learn how to transduce energies, the airplanes to remind you that you can fly. In this new world, you are telepathic, and you are seers."
- Barbara Hand Clow, *The Pleiadian Agenda*

Seeing ghosts and UFO's and experiencing the presence of angels are part of what is referred to as the "paranormal." More and more people are experiencing these phenomena as part of the Shift. The experiences can't be explained by logic, but they are real. Paranormal experiences help us break free from the conditioning of seeing only the three-dimensional Earth plane. Daniel Pinchbeck, author of *2012: The Return of Quetzalcoatl*, says that there is an "accelerating surge" in synchonicities, telepathic hints, and psychic phenomena, as well as psychophysical episodes of all types. Mayan expert Dr. Jose Arguelles notes that we are awakening from our "cultural hypnosis" and "civilizational trance."

Part of that trance involves focusing only on the physical aspects of alien contact. In her book, *Preparing for Contact*, Lyssa Royal discusses the irony of focusing on the analysis of photos of UFOs and arguing over the authenticity of sightings when there is ample evidence that people all over the world are being changed on the inside by their experiences. "This is a phenomenon that will enter the life of every human at some point in the future," she states. "The coming age requires us to be participants of contact."

In his book, *Beyond 2012: Catastrophe or Awakening?,* Geoff Stray says that alien contact is part of the spiritual shift. He says that communication between aliens and humans has been occurring more frequently, and that this is part of the acceleration of our new age. These communication experiences include dreamtime communication and altered state experiences in which communication occurs telepathically. He says that in the coming era, a mechanism inside each person will "switch on" at some point, and previously hidden knowledge will be revealed.

In many indigenous societies, that switch has never been turned off. In traditional cultures from Peru to South Dakota, tribal cultures have always accepted the "star people." Jamie Sams, a prolific Native American author, has shared the sacred teachings of indigenous societies to assist us in understanding what she refers to as the "Great Star Nation." These allies can be called upon for assistance. In *Sacred Path Cards: Discovery of Self Through Native Teachings,* she describes how she experienced "Sky Brothers and Sisters" as part of a great "Spirit Council" that enveloped her with love. The council showed her his personal records from past lives and offered to assist humanity as we move forward.

In Albuquerque, New Mexico, monthly meetings are held for people to discuss their personal experiences with UFOs, including abductions. Around 50 or 60 people attend these meetings each month. I have several friends, regular folks, who have shared their UFO experiences with me. Some see UFOs appearing over their houses on a regular basis. As a Ph.D. trained counselor, I can vouch that these are sane individuals who happen to have had extraordinary experiences in other dimensions.

I have had similar experiences. In 2004, while in a spiritual ceremony, I saw a bright white light with a blue tail blaze across the horizon barely 75-100 feet off the ground. There was no sound. As I looked at this object, I felt vibrations from other dimensions. About two years later, I was outside in the middle of the night enjoying the night sky. I saw the same light blaze above my head and over my house. What I took from these sightings was the reassurance that we are never alone, and that perhaps more will be revealed in time. For that I am grateful!

Near-Death Experiences

My client, Kay, a former 6th grade schoolteacher, is coming to terms with her own explorations in other realms of consciousness. She actually "died" when she was hit by a drunk driver ten years ago as she was biking on a dirt road near Oxford, Ohio. "I went to the Light," she said. "It was like an upside down pyramid. I saw my guardian angels. Other people were there. They told me I could stay or come back. I said that I had to go back because my mom couldn't take losing two kids. At that point my mother hadn't lost any of her four children. But six months later my brother died of a drug overdose."

Miraculously, Kay survived with no injuries to her body other than a sore knee. "I remember all these little people in the spirit world. I don't know how else to describe them. They put me back in my body and helped lift me back up on my feet. Even the wind appeared to have a face and be sentient. Along with the little people, he helped me get back on my feet."

Kay realizes that it is now her time to wake up and affirm her abilities. "I believe this was to get my attention because I absolutely was not paying attention. I knew I had psychic ability. I knew I felt things, but I was living in the dreamworld." Kay is waking up to the fact that she has healing ability in her hands (they get hot). She also realizes that she is a channel who has messages to share for the good of the people. I told her that I had seen that she was a channel in my meditation prior to our session. "Your mouth is loose for a reason," I joked. "Your purpose is about speaking and communication. Your task is to have the confidence to share the messages that come to you. What people do with those messages is up to them."

Kay is embracing her gifts fully. She's received messages about future Earth changes, pole shifts, and where we might be headed. When I told her that others have received messages similar to hers, including tribal elders and wisdom keepers, she was relieved. Simply knowing that others are experiencing similar things has made her more confident. Kay's story can teach us that we are never alone. I extend gratitude to Kay for embracing herself and to Spirit for allowing the experience to be shared.

If you are interested in near-death experience research, you can read thousands of reports at the Near Death Experience Research Foundation. Check out the website at NDERF.org. Excellent research on near-death experiences has been done by Dr. Kenneth Ring, author of *The Omega Project*, and Dr. Raymond Moody, who wrote *Life After Life*. Both of these spiritual pioneers have made it their life purpose to study and share the hopeful message that human consciousness does indeed transcend physical death.

Angel Experiences and Channeling

What makes something real? Must it have physical form? Must we be able to see it? Because we've never set foot in Russia, does that mean the country doesn't exist? Using a similar analogy, angels may operate, for the most part, outside of the frame of a camera lens. Perhaps this is why there may be resistance by some to the notion of their very existence. And yet many of us are experiencing them as important spiritual guides and messengers. A spate of popular bestselling books from authors such as Doreen Virtue and Sylvia Browne show the tremendous interest of the public in the subject. Angels are "as close to the Divine as we can get," says author Ambika Wauters, author of *The Angel Oracle: Working with the Angels for Guidance, Inspiration, and Love*. She references the work of Meister Eckhart, who said that an angel is simply an "idea of God."

Albert Einstein said, "All knowledge of reality starts from experience, and ends in it." This is certainly true for angel experiences. Whether or not you feel this energy, trust that the angels and Archangels, as a representation of the Divine, are there and will respond to your call. They hear you and will respond to your invocation and calling in. And how they respond to the call is different for everyone. The act of asking is an amplifier of angel energy. The more you ask, the more the energy will come to you. This process of asking and then receiving is one form of what is known as spiritual channeling.

The notion of spiritual channeling perhaps might be a bit off-putting for some, seemingly only for those who are seasoned psychics or have some supernatural ability. Nothing could be further from the truth. We all have the ability to channel. It's a form of engaging our creativity. Anyone can "channel," so you don't have to be a psychic or healer to do it! If I want to use my creativity to channel spirits, then I can do that. If I want to use my creativity to channel a fabulous new recipe, then I may want to do that. If I want to use my creativity to channel a song or write a book, I have that option. I believe that channeling is engaging our creativity to manifest something from the heavens and bring it down to Earth.

It is completely up to us to decide what we want to channel. I dabbled in channeling spiritual messages for the purposes of a potential book before deciding that it wasn't for me. Pretty soon, I was listening to others in my head so much that I wasn't living life as myself! I didn't want to live that way, so I asked those voices to stop, and they did.

One word of caution about channeling spirits: that form of channeling is not to be undertaken lightly. When we channel spirits, sometimes lower vibratory spirits can appear, and it requires a tremendous amount of clarity, light, and opening in order to have the wisdom to properly handle this. Even if you're clean and open, you don't always know who or what will show up. You don't just open your home and invite anyone into your kitchen, do you? In much the same way, it would be somewhat incredulous for you to open the doors of your house (for example, your body and mind) for anyone and everyone to come in and have a seat at your table. It is wise to be selective. If you decide to allow this to happen, it would be wise to have a spiritual mentor, and invoke the protection of guardian spirits. I use the energy of Archangel Michael for this purpose. He is the one of the sword whose job is to eliminate darkness. If you don't resonate with Archangel Michael, that's fine. Choose a symbol or figure that will protect you and in whom you can place your faith and trust (Quan Yin, Mother Mary, Kali, etc.).

Psychokinesis: Mind over Matter

The origin of "psychokinesis" is from the Latin "psyche," which means "mind," and "kinesis," which means "motion." Thus, the literal translation of this common phrase is 'mind causing motion.'

I often ask my coaching clients to use their creativity and intention to affect matter. We're all electrical, and we're all energy. Quantum physics has demonstrated this. The subject has been popularized by books on the Law of Attraction, such as *The Secret*. We are waking up to the fact that every thought, no matter how small, affects matter.

The only question is how long it will take for that thought to manifest. If we focus on pleasant thoughts, our existence will be pleasant. If we focus on negative thoughts, constantly in a state of worry or internal pressure, this will manifest as combustion in the body. We literally can cause disease within ourselves. Navigating our way through this new age involves realizing our power to affect matter.

One example of psychokinesis is when we enlarge our energy fields to such a degree that it affects the electrical components around us. One of the effects of the Shift is that as the Earth's magnetic poles are being altered, so is our ability to hold charge. As the three-dimensional world merges with the vibrations of higher dimensions, we pass back and forth between worlds.

Our auras are becoming larger to support the expansion. We are able to contain more in our energy fields. Because we are able to "hold more charge," this sometimes disrupts the computers, tablets, phones, and fax machines around us!

My friend, Raline Starc, who has contributed to the epilogue of this book, sent me the following email regarding her experiences with psychokinesis—in particular, electrical psychokinesis:

I grew up having an effect on the television and radio (they would turn off/on at random whenever I focused on them or just walked by) but after a while it calmed down. I got my first "taste" of telekinesis in action at a very young age when I saw a relative shatter a plate in anger without even touching it. That is when I understood what I was doing and was capable of as well, so I tried to dull the impetus as much as I can.

Yesterday a co-worker was complaining about how much pain she was in. She said jokingly, "Just put me out of my misery, this pain won't go away." I replied, "Well if you want I could make everything stop." I was looking at the power outlet at the precise moment that I said it. (She knows a little about me and told me afterward she was glad I was not looking at her!)

In that instant everything on that power line died. Both our computers, the heaters, and one of the printers. The lights were still on, the fax machine and other printer were still running, and no other office in the building was affected. I called Information Technology and also Maintenance but to no avail; what had been done needed the "big dogs" to come in and fix it.

In the last year my effect on electrical components has been increasing at quite a clip. The following are still not working correctly: my car, my cellphone, my laptop (completely fried), myself (I am constantly being shocked all the time). I have had to neutralize myself by carefully monitoring what I eat and drink and think and of course be very selective about clothing and footwear so I don't combust. Ha! Anybody else have these issues?

In answer to your question, Raline, yes! Recently, I was on the phone with a first-time client, Kevin, and some large angelic spirits entered into the process. This happens with most clients, and yet it was especially strong this time as I opened my third eye and asked that

Kevin's be opened as well. I could feel the presence of angels clearing the way for a powerful energy healing with Kevin.

Those feelings were affirmed the moment I pressed the green "Talk" button on my phone. I was only able to get out the words, "I'm so excited to talk to you!" before the phone went dead. It wasn't just the line that got cut off. The *phone* was 100 percent fried. Toast. Thankfully, I have several backups because this happens with some frequency.

Once Kevin and I re-established our connection. he told me that as my phone went dead, the power in his office building went out. He said, "I've always been a high-energy guy." Clearly!

Eventually, Kevin experienced excitement and relief in finding his true self, and communion and reunion with the Divine. As we were speaking, I could sense the angels playing with and fine-tuning the energy vibration. They wanted to go higher. Yet to do so would have caused the phones to be completely fried. Ironically, Kevin works in the telecommunications industry. He offered to send me special equipment and headphones that may better hold the charge of the spiritual energy.

The point of including stories about energy influence is twofold: first, to notice when such events happen in your own life; and second, to embrace these as *real* experiences, not coincidences.

When energy moves profoundly like this, Spirit is always trying to get our attention!

Seven-day Psychokinetic Exercises:

1. *Create Goosebumps.* Creating goosebumps at will is an example of psychokinesis. The ability to produce them will depend on the strength of the frequency you are able to carry in your nervous system. The more charge you hold, the more you will be able to influence processes like goosebumps that are controlled by the unconscious autonomic nervous system. Whenever I do remote energy work with clients, for 60 minutes I am in a state of near-constant goosebumps. This happens like clockwork. Because I do so much of this work, my nervous system has adapted. I can now create goosebumps at will. I believe that you, too, can do this.

Each day for the next 7 days, for 10 minutes per day do this exercise. As you lie in bed in the morning or at night, simply "feel" the goosebumps on your arm. Make the imagined sensations as real as possible. Before long it won't be imagined anymore, it will be real! When this happens, you'll believe in your power all the more.

2. *Energize Your Plants.* Each day for 7 days, send love to your plants. As you gently touch a plant, imagine it thriving and growing larger than ever. Imagine a spark of light energy coming out of your fingertips, penetrating the plant, going to its core. When you water your plants, use water that has been charged with your intention for about 1 minute prior to application.

Water is a living organism that is receptive to every thought. It becomes imprinted with our energy and intentions. Shamans have worked with this for thousands of years. In the late 1700's, Franz Mesmer (whose name is the root of "mesmerize"), was one of the first modern scientists to discover that water can be charged with healing properties. For added "before and after" effect, take a picture of your plants both prior to and after your psychokinesis work. If you do this exercise with intention and devotion for 7 days, you will notice a distinct difference in the quality of the plants.

3. *Covert-Op Healing.*   This is one of my favorite psychokinetic exercises because it involves an amusing "sleight of hand." Covert-Op Healing involves sending energy to others without their knowledge and watching their reaction.

My friend, L.D. Porter, (LDIntuitive.com), a God-gifted distance healer with an uncanny ability for psychokinesis, says, "You don't need someone's permission to pray for them." He's right. I invite you to take his advice to heart and use psychokinesis on your family or loved ones. It can be even more profound if you do this exercise with someone who is challenging for you or who is involved in detrimental behavior.

Each day, for 7 days, take at least 10 minutes to send loving energy into someone's energy field. (Reiki practitioners should already be adept at this practice.) This can occur as you speak to the person or as you are sitting around together. They key is to "charge yourself up" with love energy, and then ask the Divine presence to send that energy to the person. After each "treatment," make a mental or physical notation of how their behavior changes. For even more fun, you might reveal to your friend or loved one that you will be doing this exercise, but don't tell them exactly when you're doing it. Revealing this much will probably spark them to become more in tune with their own energy. It can also allow you to educate them about the power of psychokinesis, especially if they notice an effect from your intentions and prayers for them.

Exploring Outer Realms of Consciousness

Other fascinating subjects are coming to light, including Lemuria, Atlantis, and crystal skulls. People who have near-death experiences, angel experiences, and experiences with other dimensions are explorers in the outer edge of consciousness. We are excited about learning more, but to function optimally on the Earth plane, we must examine our motivations for wanting to know more.

One reason why people do not have paranormal experiences is that they aren't yet ready. Our ego could be shocked prematurely, and actually could cause some of us, depending on our wiring, to become psychotic.

Whatever you pray for, whatever you intend, know your reasons for asking. Do you want to tell good stories? Are you just curious? Or do you want to use those experiences in order to understand the Web of Life? Will you use your experiences to help others?

Spirit reveals information only when the time is right, and especially if your motivation is primarily to help others. Your time will come if it is meant to be. Don't rush psychic experiences. And be careful about desiring intuitive development simply for the ego gratification.

If you do have psychic experiences, keep those experiences "sacred" for awhile before sharing them with others or broadcasting them on social media. Certain experiences are meant just for you. Be vigilant about what to share and what not to share.

And be careful what you wish for! The power of our thoughts and intentions is increasing, and our ability to manifest on the Earth plane is quickening.

Chapter Six

Dealing Effectively With Your Ascension Experiences

As the Earth's frequency changes, so do our bodies—the ones we are aware of (mental, emotional, spiritual, physical) and those we are not (the quantum field). Over the past several years you may have noticed changes in your energy system. These changes are tied to the Earth's magnetic field because the way your body reacts is largely due to the way the Earth reacts.

If you type the phrase "Ascension Symptoms" into any search engine, you will get a variety of information. I don't like this term because the word "symptoms" comes from a medical model that implies that something is wrong. Nothing is wrong. Yes, the Ascension may hurt, but for only one reason: those who are spiritually sensitive are experiencing the darkness on its way out! The universe is shining more Light on us and that causes anything not in line with that Light to move out. Because this movement is positive, I believe it is more accurate to call these "ascension experiences".

Here are some common experiences:

Feeling like you are going crazy. This feeling is quite common. You are actually becoming more sane, but it *feels* like you are going crazy. Spirit is giving the Earth and its vibration the equivalent of a chiropractic adjustment. If you've ever had a spinal adjustment, you know that immediately following, your body can feel strange and out of balance. You are experiencing the world from a more balanced place, yet at first it feels strange. In much the same way, immediately after the Earth plane gets an adjustment, we may feel disoriented and awkward. We may think that something is wrong, but this is just an erroneous assumption of the ego. You can take comfort in the fact that many of us are feeling disoriented, and these feelings are not to be judged. They are simply to be accepted. Learning to embrace feelings of going crazy and reframe them as "going sane" is a healthy way to advance spiritually in our new era.

Weight fluctuation unrelated to food consumption. One common but under-reported cause of weight gain is related to spiritual advancement. There is a reason why the happy buddha is depicted as round and fat. The more we advance spiritually, the more energy (e.g. mass) we can hold in our energy body and physical body. Many of us protect ourselves from the world through additional fat or body mass. The nervous system does this for us. It's not necessarily unconscious. It's actually done with full consciousness, although it's the body that is conscious, not the mind. The body will do everything in its power to protect us and serve our greater good. If it senses that we are quite sensitive to other people's energy or to spiritual energy in general, it may begin to accumulate fat to protect us. Is this a good thing? We must remove any Western bias to answer that question. Simply be aware that there may be a deeper reason for your weight gain, and that reason has nothing to do with bodily dysfunction. Your body knows best. Once you can accept that, you are well on your way to accepting yourself, whether you perceive extra weight to be a problem or not.

Mysterious food cravings. Have you had any unusual or unexplained cravings for certain foods? I always crave pickles after intense spiritual work. There is something in the food that helps me clear out energy. Perhaps it's the vinegar and salt—after all, they are both astringents that absorb and clean. Vinegar is a household cleaner and salt is an astringent that soaks up not only water, but negative energy as well. Having spiritual energy running through our bodies alters our energy system and can manifest as food cravings. For more information on why this might be the case, be the good spiritual detective that you are and Google for additional information. If you're craving cherries, for instance, you will learn that cherries have long been a bronchial dilator that allows the body to take in more breath and energy.

Dizziness or disorientation. Whenever I quickly stand up from a seated position, I seem to be able to connect with the higher realms. It's as if I temporarily leave my body for 1-2 seconds and everything goes black. Sometimes I fall to the ground or clutch objects so that I don't fall and hurt myself. While most physicians would write this off to low blood pressure when moving from being seated to standing, I am aware that when this happens, I lose ordinary consciousness. It's as if I am "watching" myself. Everything goes quiet. Sometimes I have the odd sensation of depersonalization, in which I seem to lose my identity as Michael and connect with the heavens. If these feelings of dizziness or disorientation happen to you, notice when it occurs, and then be sure to embrace these feelings not as a disorder, but as a sign that you are indeed advancing spiritually. You are an in-tune instrument, being played by the heavens! And be sure to stand up slowly!

Sleep disruptions and waking up in the middle of the night. While much sleep disruption can be due to bodily changes as we age, there is no denying that energetic changes will affect consciousness at various points during the night: Three o'clock, for instance, is a time period of peak energy flow, both a.m. and p.m. Many indigenous elders start their ceremonies around 3:00 p.m. because this is a sacred time, a polarity marker in which the energies help us get closer to God. The same holds true for 3:00 a.m. This is when other energies are at their highest and may affect the ability to sleep. Rather than fight it, learn to accept it as a natural part of spiritual change. If you can't sleep, get up and do something creative or productive as a means of coping. On the other hand, you may experience periods of intense sleep during the day. This, again, is natural. It's one of the body's ways of handling energy changes and recharging.

Feeling of increased pressure as if you are about to explode. This is a result of the higher frequencies pushing up against your darker areas. To cope with the higher frequencies, we need to attend spiritual ceremonies, healing classes, and community events. If we aren't doing this regularly, we will feel Spirit tugging on us through a feeling of pressure. These high vibrations are asking us to move, literally! One of the best to handle this is to physically move through dancing, hiking, biking, or martial arts so that you are better grounded and more comfortable in your body and can sweat out the energy you no longer need.

Heightened sensitivity. This is the focus of my coaching work with people who identify themselves as highly sensitive. There is a whole class of people who fall into this category, as we have described in Chapter 4. Heightened senses of smell, touch, taste, hearing and vision are common. You may also experience bodily aches and pains intensifying, especially when you are in groups. There is nothing you can do to lessen your sensitivity, although you can certainly use the healthy methods described below to cope with this sensitivity.

Emotional ups and downs accompanied by bouts of crying. Many of us are experiencing emotional earthquakes in which the terrain of our emotions is altered. Emotions have a way of rubbing up against us when either great darkness or great Light is shown upon them. There is a special place in your body where emotion is stored. The divine wisdom of your body will decide where exactly that is for you, and yet for many of us, unprocessed emotion can be stored in the second chakra area. This additional emotional energy may affect the lower back, the kidney area, the sacrum, and the hip area. If you experience pain or discomfort in these areas, your body is asking for additional grounding and discharge support (see the methods in this chapter for how to clear energy).

Telepathy and other unexplained psychic experiences. You may hear words and phrases being spoken into your ear. You might see strange blips of unexplained energy or colors in your field of vision. I hear sometimes crazy-sounding phrases at the oddest times. Do I need to know the meaning of these words? Not really, unless they come up again and again. Then I use my spiritual detective skills to ask for more information. You may also be especially sensitive to these telepathic experiences when you are in quiet moments with your partner or loved ones.

Coping With the Ascension and Higher Frequencies

Since a hallmark of our new age is increased vibration, it naturally follows that our strategies for coping are energetic in nature. Learning how to cope with energy was a primary topic of my first book, *The Complete Empath Toolkit*. (For more in-depth information about how energy works and moves, refer to this book.) For now, I will list some effective strategies for making our lives on the Earth plane more comfortable.

A principle of energy is that it never dissipates, it just changes. It moves from one person to another, from one place to another, from one body to another. The primary conduit is the Earth, which allows the energy to move. For example, when lightning moves from the clouds downward, it must have an Earth ground in order to discharge. In the same way, we must be grounded to the Earth's energy in order to get rid of the energy that we no longer need. If we're not grounded in our body, then discharging lower vibratory energy is difficult.

Learning how the body discharges energy is important in these new times. The body has its own Divine consciousness that will naturally try to expel energy that is no longer necessary. It attempts to remain in homeostasis—a state of equilibrium and balance.

Here is a partial list of ways that old energy discharges from the body in an attempt to remain in homeostasis:

Tears
Coughing
Sneezing
Menstruation
Sweating
Gas
Rapid eye movement
Trembling or shaking

Bursts of laughter
Stomach growling
Diarrhea
Urination
Vomiting
Burping
Spit production
Kidney stones
Rashes or Pus formation

What is modern society's reaction to the bodily functions listed above? Might these be considered by some to be unacceptable or "gross?" Rather than seeing these body functions as being completely natural and controlled by a divine consciousness that is outside of our awareness, many have been taught to look upon them as problems or symptoms. With this judgment, we have been conditioned to do the exact opposite of what the body requires. We suck in our bellies, we repress the natural urge to cough, and we don't cry when we need to. It's crazy and backwards.

And what's the bottom line of all this holding in? Much preventable illness, perhaps even including some energy based syndromes such as chronic fatigue or fibromyalgia (depending on the individual, of course).

We've been trained, erroneously, to believe that certain aspects of our bodies are shameful. Gaseous discharges, belching, and the like are how the body processes and transmutes energy. I don't know why air comes up and out of my esophagus at times, and I don't need to know. I just desire to honor the wisdom of my body and simply exist. If that means I belch, laugh uncontrollably, cry uncontrollably, and make others socially uncomfortable, well, then I will allow my body to do it, regardless of what others might think.

Often our energy input is too much for the body to handle, so we can assist it in achieving balance. In the following pages, I will share with you some highly effective techniques. The key is to achieve bodily balance and harmony, which promotes psychic balance and harmony.

This harmony is becoming the default state of our new age.

Techniques for Grounding.

Sage and smudging. Any form of sage and/or sweetgrass will do wonders for keeping your energy field clean. These medicinal plants have been harvested and used by indigenous cultures for thousands of years. You don't have to know why these work. Grab any form of sage or sweetgrass, even cedar, and light it with a match. Take the smoke and use it to surround your body, running it through your energy field. If it's not unpleasant, directly inhale it (you may immediately cough, which is a good sign that it's working!) and pray to the spirit of the plant to heal you and keep you protected. Plants are living creatures with consciousness. Even if the plant itself is "dead," the spirit of the plant will respond, offering assistance in energy clearing.

Stones. Stones and crystals are the oldest material on Earth. As such, they contain all of the power and energy of recorded Earthly history. Recently I was watching a C-Span documentary on the White House. The historians marveled at how old the furniture and paintings were, and how visitors get such a thrill to walk in the same room as Abraham Lincoln. I got a little chuckle, because while Thomas Jefferson's imported china plates are certainly interesting, if you want to experience the thrill of being in the presence of true history and something *really* old, all you have to do is go out into the street and pick up a rock or pebble! Or better yet, go touch a mountain rock. You won't find anything older than that.

Some of the better stones used to promote grounding are the black ones: tourmaline, obsidian, and onyx. These stones repel negative energy. Smoky quartz, amber, and vanadinite are also excellent for grounding. Conversely, if you want to promote a connection to the heavens, turquoise, amethyst, and lapis are stones that help with this. Like plants, stones are creatures who are alive. They vibrate, albeit slowly. Also like plants, the spirit of the "stone people" will assist you in taking away energy that you don't need. Just like indigenous cultures do by using stones as a primary tool of the sweat lodge, you can call on the spirit of the stones to take from you that which no longer serves you. Because energy does accumulate in stones, be sure to clean your stones every few weeks. The easiest way to do this is to set the stones outside in a crystal container of water and salt to get 8-10 hours of direct sunshine. You may also elect to bury them overnight in the ground a few times a year.

Energy technology. Wonderful new energy technologies will assist you in discharging energy and promoting grounding. Devices such as the Rife machine or EPFX/SCIO quantum biofeedback can be amazing tools that will generate frequencies and send those frequencies into your aura and your body. There are also energy shielding devices such as the BioElectric Shield (use coupon code 'empaths' for a 10% discount) that are designed to protect the body from electromagnetic interference. Not everyone's energy field is the same, so exploring energy technology is a trial and error process. There are no guarantees or absolutes when it comes to the claims of some of these energy devices. And yet, they can be beneficial methods of coping.

Mud baths. Many spas offer these services. If you don't want to pay exorbitant sums for these treatments, simply go down to a marsh or lake and submerge yourself into as much mud as possible. It might feel awkward, but the mud will ground you and discharge unneeded energy. The mud, when allowed to dry, will act as an astringent and suck a lot of negative energy out of you. This is a method used by indigenous shamans in many cultures throughout the world. If it's winter, get a bowl, fill it with dirt, add a little water, and use the mud on your body. Then you can wash it off in the bathtub or shower.

Sea salt. Salt is an astringent. It pulls moisture and other subtle energy into itself. It's also a preservative—not only for food, but for your energetic sanity. You can strategically place little bowls of salt in the corners of your house or office. Change the bowls every few weeks to clear out the energy. If you can, use sea salt, which is generally more effective and natural than processed salt.

Diet. There are so many harmful processed chemicals in food that we need to be conscious and responsible in choosing what goes into our bodies. Many of us crave meat to stay grounded. That certainly is an option and may be necessary for some. The vibration of meat, especially red meat or pork, is lower than most other food. There's a reason why Jewish people are cautioned against pork, and although I am not a theologian, I would proffer that it has something to do with a pig's energetic vibration. Constant ingestion of meat, especially processed meat, will lower your vibration. There are no hard and fast rules in our new age, though, and so you must find what works for you. In general, the best grounding foods are those grown under the Earth (potatoes, beets, carrots, etc).

Many people believe that drinking coffee is an indulgence or unhealthy. While every person's body reacts differently, coffee is generally helpful for the body because it has a laxative effect that allows us to get rid of energy we don't need. Some tribal societies refer to coffee as "black medicine." There's a reason why colon hydrotherapists use coffee in their treatments. It allows the intestines to discharge energy we don't need. If you're sensitive to caffeine, try decaffeinated coffee. While tea may not offer the laxative effect of coffee, it has other benefits. Research has shown that both green and black tea drinkers may be protected from heart disease through a lowering of cholesterol and blood pressure.

Bodywork and energy work. Taking care of your body by allowing it to feel touch is vitally important. The manual manipulation of tissue and fluid promotes better circulation and breathing. When the body is touched through massage and other therapies, it secretes seratonin, the feel-good chemical that is nature's natural anti-depressant. Beyond everyone's favorite, Swedish massage, there are other excellent forms of bodywork. These include polarity therapy, Feldenkrais, ortho-bionomy, and if you love stretching, Thai massage or shiatsu. All of these modalities promote better blood circulation, better nutrient absorption, better immune system response, and invocation of the body's relaxation response.

Exercise. In the new age, vigorous physical exercise is becoming less of a choice and more of a requirement in order to keep ourselves thriving. Even though it's an old quote from 1873, it still applies today. "Those who think they have not time for exercise," said Edward Stanley, "will sooner or later have to find time for illness." Beyond the typical cardiovascular work, techniques such as Nia and Zumba are gaining in popularity because they are not only helpful, but fun. The Nia technique is a blend of yoga and martial arts done to a variety of music that encourages bodily and personal expression. Zumba is popular for its emphasis on training the body's core (abs and hips). Like Nia, it is done to music—in this case, Latin-infused grooves.

Any form of movement will promote grounding, especially movement that cleanses the energy system through sweat production, and especially movement that uses the feet. Yoga has been used for centuries to align the body and mind and to adjust the body's subtle energies. It promotes grounding and a quieting of the ego probably better than any other physical exercise. And the great thing is that it can be learned in groups, which amplify the healing power, and at home. If you're intimidated by going to the gym, simply move wherever you are. The Nintendo Wii has a very good workout program called "Wii Fit," which, along with its balance board, makes exercise fun and accessible. I have found that it is a surprisingly effective way to learn yoga. It can be done on your own time, at your own pace, and has a built-in rewards system that gives points based on performance.

Infrared devices and sweat lodges. Just as tears are cleansing agents that take away unneeded energy, so is sweat. Many infrared devices (both mats and saunas) are available today. This technology comes primarily from Asia where it is used to treat cancer and other serious health problems. The infrared rays penetrate the body more deeply than traditional heating pads and temporarily raise the body's core temperature. The BioMat is one of the better products on the market. I have used mine since 2007 with success and it's one of the best purchases I have ever made. Whatever energies I take on from others get scrubbed away with infrared rays that promote the body's metabolism and excretion through urine, the intestines, and, especially, body sweat. The Native American sweat lodge is also a tool for healing that detoxifies through sweat. However, these lodges are harder to find. Information about sweat lodge ceremonies is typically through word of mouth and you would likely need a personal invitation.

Spending time in nature. Being in nature helps us resonate more closely with the slower frequency of the Earth's field. When we touch the ground with our bare skin, free electrons enter the body to reduce inflammation, and we are able to discharge energy into the Earth itself. You can lie with your stomach touching the ground and do the yogic asana "child's pose" to enhance this process. Ask the Earth to take the energy you don't need. Imagine the energy leaving through your umbilical cord area. Trees also absorb energy by pulling it from us (it does not hurt the tree as trees thrive on our 'waste,' which includes carbon dioxide). The result is more grounded energy. There is also a significant reason Jesus went to the mountains to pray. When you spend time in the mountains, you raise your vibration. Not only do you get the benefits of living at high altitudes (a more resistant heart, increased red blood cell production, and a leaner body), but you are actually "closer" to the Divine.

Rattles and tuning forks. Some of the tools used in indigenous ceremonies are the fan, the rattle, and the drum. These are effective in breaking up energy, literally, and to move it around. A drum is played ceremonially, not just because it sounds good. It is played intentionally because the sonic boom of the drum not only is attuned to deep Earth energy but also breaks up pockets of stagnant energy in our bodies. It's a similar principle to using lasers to remove tumors in western medicine. Using our vibrational tools, we focus on where there's too much energy and we use these techniques of vibration to move the energy out.

These techniques take many forms, including using tuning forks, rattles, Tibetan or Crystal bowls, drums, the human voice, and other cultural instruments that shake up energy and get it moving. A simple hand clap is enough to move energy. When we clap our hands as a way of applauding someone, we are doing two things. First, we are extending loud, crisp sound waves that move throughout the room to break up energy and get it moving. Second, we are activating the energy meridians in our own bodies, especially as a way of opening the minor chakras that are located in the center of the hands. You may not have thought of it as such, and yet clapping is a spiritual experience designed to raise everyone's vibration.

Those cultures that stomp their feet instead of clapping understand and promote this same principle. (It just wouldn't be the same if we tapped our noses)! I sometimes clap during my Inner Power Coaching sessions with clients to get my own energy moving, and I will sometimes ask clients to do the same. It's a simple way to clear energy. Although they are designed for pianos, tuning forks offer similar benefits and can be sampled at new age expos or purchased online. When babies shake rattles, they move energy out of their fields and become soothed as well.

It may appear mystical or intimidating to see aboriginal dancers with their hands thrown to the sky dancing to the drum in ceremonies such as the Sun Dance ceremony. There certainly is mysticism and spiritual connection involved; however, on a more practical and scientific level, these aboriginal dance ceremonies are harnessing the power of large amounts of sound waves to expel energy in places where there is too much of it (in our heads or our blocked heart chakras).

Energy Tapping. This is my modified protocol based on the Emotional Freedom Technique (EFT), a well-documented method of energy medicine developed by Gary Craig and Roger Callahan that opens meridians to help permanently eliminate trauma or other unwanted states. Techniques similar to this have been taught in some form by Callahan and Craig since the 1980's.

Individuals have used EFT with varying degrees of success. I find that it is temporarily useful for myself, while some of my clients and colleagues have reported that energy meridian tapping has permanently cured unwanted emotional states. Below is a modification of the more effective protocols that I have encountered over the years. Please remember that these are *not* the Emotional Freedom Techniques, but are based on the principle that energy can move when our meridians are open.

Perform each of these protocols for 10 to 15 seconds each, in the following order. Use them when you feel ungrounded, when anxiety arises, or some other unwanted emotional state is giving you problems.

1. Tap the bone beneath your eyes.
2. Tap the spot in the center above your mouth and below your nose.
3. Tap the point(s) where the collarbone forms, right above your sternum.
4. Tap the sides of the left and right rib cages, underneath the arms.
5. Tap the "karate chop point" underneath the padding of your hand. This is the point that would connect with the surface if you were going to karate chop a block of wood.

Essential Oils. The essential oils of herbs and flowers are some of the highest vibrating life extracts known to man. Lavender and patchouli calm the nervous system and citronella repels negative energy. Lemon, peppermint, and orange have uplifting qualities and stimulate energy flow. The effectiveness of any of the essential oils is largely due to personal preferences. Honor what feels right to you. Go to your local health food store and smell some of these essences. Experiment with the particular energies and scents in each bottle. These stimulate the olfactory areas of the brain, release seratonin, and allow you to relax into your softer, gentler, truer self.

Body Positions. The Asian cultures know the power and medicine that is contained in the squatting position. Dr. Randolph Stone, the founder of Polarity Therapy, was a pioneer who brought the squat back from those cultures and integrated it into Western energy medicine.

Dr. Stone's research that spanned his 60-year medical career showed that the squat is the healthiest position for the body. It gives the organs a good massage, stretches the muscles of the back, releases gas, and promotes good digestion. I am convinced that if we all squatted more, the incidences of chronic digestive conditions such as irritable bowel syndrome would be greatly reduced.

Give it a try; start gently at first. Then see if you can rest your armpits on top of your knees and remain balanced for several minutes. If you can't do this, don't worry. It would be a nice goal to work toward. As an added benefit, sitting in this position on a daily basis will allow you to build up your lower leg muscles and ankle muscles. Simply move the body up and down for 30 seconds to a minute each day in this position. This exercise has the added benefit of promoting grounding. Having strong leg muscles is an important factor in the ability to ground to the Earth energy.

Every morning when rising and starting your day, do the squat for just 1 to 2 minutes. It will help you to start your bowel movement and bring regularity to your energy. That way, you won't have to rely so much on over-the-counter supplements that contain chemicals that actually may interfere with your energy.

Harnessing Sacred Space. Space is an important and often overlooked tool. It is a powerful ally in your quest for spiritual, earthly, and energetic balance. Space can be created in the joints. It can be created in the house. It can be created in relationships. The more you focus on the intention of bringing in space, the more free and less cramped you will feel. Simply imagining space being created in between the spinal vertebrae is a powerful meditation that will allow for more energy flow.

If your mental space is starting to feel old and dusty, simply changing your physical space will allow more energy. Everything is related. Every small part (microcosm) is a reflection of the whole (macrocosm). Eliminating clutter in one part of your life (the physical) will also eliminate clutter in another part of your life (the mental body). So, when you unclutter your desk or living space every now and then, you will find that the circumstances of your life will reflect that change. All of us can and will benefit from using principles of managing space to improve our energy and environment.

Many exciting discoveries are coming our way. Our new age is teaching us to live more fully in balance and harmony with the heavens and with the Earth. By following the guidelines in this chapter and by making the exercises in this book a regular part of your spiritual practice, you will begin to thrive in ways you never thought possible.

Writing this book has been a labor of love, and I am honored that you have chosen to read it. May you be an inspiration to all those around you. May you tap into deep reservoirs of goodwill as you move toward hope, health, healing and Light. I end this book with one of my favorite phrases and pray that it finds you full of peace, joy, and serenity.

Onward!

Epilogue: Personal Dialogues on The Shift

To close this book, I sent an open invitation to my empath clients, my newsletter readers, and my healing practitioner friends to share their perspectives surrounding the Shift and spiritual transformation. The following responses illustrate the divinity and powerful perception that each of us have. They have been edited only for clarity.

Just as each of us is part of God, each of these passages are little nuggets of spiritual gold that contain a delicious reflection of, and connection to, spiritual truth. It's a little bit like sampling a box of chocolates. Each has a unique flavor, just like you! So grab a cup of coffee or tea, and savor the richness and flavor of these premium grade A reflections.

WHAT DOES THE SHIFT MEAN TO YOU?

~~~~

I believe it is the beginning of a NEW time. I feel this shift is a time for us to transform from old relationship models to a new one. As an empath, intuitive, teacher and speaker, I have experienced in my professional and personal life, as well, a sense—a real universal soul calling to redefine what we currently know about relationships. We have reached a plateau of interacting with others via the status quo. Our interactions thus far, as we can clearly see and feel have created much pain in our lives not only individually but also collectively. Why? Because we have been seeking to either fill something in us we believe to be missing, desire to find someone to complete, fix or save us. The point is we have been looking outside of ourselves for way too long. We have been blaming others, pointing the finger, and looking across the street to see who hurt us. But the time is now to look in the mirror to see who is really creating our pain. To see the one that is creating and attracting drama in our lives. We can no longer avoid ourselves.

The shift is our wake up call. It is our spiritual alarm clock gnawing at us to do what we came to do here on earth - to heal and nurture ourselves at our core. It is about finally looking in the mirror and seeing ourselves completely and fully. This is the time for us to take responsibility for our actions - for ourselves. The world is merely a mirror of who we are on the inside. In order for us to change our world, we must be willing to change it from the inside.

How do we do that? By loving ourselves, and accepting every ounce of us, including our shadows – the side that makes us cringe. This is the side we hide with much desperation but it always finds its way to display itself every chance it gets. Obviously it has because look at what we have created in our world thus far – the wars, starvation, market crashes, high unemployment rates, increasing divorces, crumbling businesses, environmental disasters, sky rocketing mental, physical and emotional diseases, etc. These are all just public displays of our insides vomited outward. This is the very essence of us that we condemn and chastise in someone else.

The moment is now for us to heal our world, our relationships by taking responsibility for ourselves through healing, loving and accepting ourselves. Imagine a world where everyone loved them self unconditionally. Imagine how each of these people would treat their neighbors and their Earth. We can no longer ignore ourselves – our souls are lovingly not going to allow it.

I view the shift as a portal to unconditional love. The love we all are searching for in each of our relationships. The old relationship model of owning someone, looking to them to fill us in some way, is shifting to unconditional love relationships. This will require us to heal and learn a new way of being. This new way of being is about complete vulnerability and emotionally intimacy with us. It means looking in the mirror with new lenses. Seeing all of our beauty – not just what we believe to be beautiful or want to see as beautiful but all that shadow side that makes us cringe. It means completely loving and accepting the pieces of us we judge as unacceptable – all of our perfect imperfections. And my role in this shift is to help each person to see who they really are and love every ounce of it. My intention and reason for being here on earth at this time and doing what I do is to teach people how to relate to others by learning how to relate with themselves first. It was one of the hardest lessons I have had to learn but the most rewarding. I have not only changed my life but am completely loving and living it the way I deserve to live it. And by living my life this way I know I am not only changing my life but the world I live in and every life I touch.

- Trinity Nieves is a Board Certified Holistic Health Practitioner, Spiritual Life and Positive Psychology Coach, Ordained Minister, Neuro-Linguistic Programmer, Reiki Master/Teacher and Quantum Touch Practitioner. Trinity has a private practice helping clients to create what they desire and facilitates workshops across New Jersey and New York. Trinity also distributes a weekly Love Yourself! Inspirational email newsletter. www.TrinityNieves.com

~~~~~

The Dawn of a New Era Begins with You

The shift means celebration! It is the ending of a very long era, and the dance of life that heralds the dawn of peace, prosperity, compassion, harmony and being our authentic selves. It is vital now to remain strongly anchored in Divine Love. As our connection to Source becomes stronger we have less and less need for fear. If we really look at the problems in our world, much of it is due to fear or greed. In other words, it is because of a lack of trust in our Divine Connection.

What is needed and this shift offers us, is enormous opportunity for change and to honor our authentic self and the God/Goddess within us all. Right now many people are resisting the call to change by clinging to old patterns of belief. This is their choice. However, the opportunity is here for all to decide to become a happier, more joyful person. With trust in our Divine Connection there is strength and courage to know that we are worthy, truly worthy of love and a joyful life on earth.

As a healer, writer and artist, my wish is for you to know that you are divinely loved. I ask you to dance in the celebration of this immense opportunity for life-altering change that heralds a new era which is Heaven on Earth. You are worthy of love and happiness. Right here. Right now. What would our life be like without fear? How would our life transform with the complete knowing that life is meant to be a dance of joy? What would it take for you to make a commitment to happiness? Struggle or joy. What do you choose?

- Maggie Terry Viale is co-author of *Happiness Awaits You!* a collection of 68 true stories by 44 authors. It began with her desire to bring more happiness into the world. She realized that loss and other life changing events often cause us to lose sight of the people and things that bring us joy.   www.HappinessAwaitsYou.info

~~~~~

I am a professional astrologer of many years, a spiritual counselor and healer, and a sound healing practitioner and teacher. I have always been an empath who is more attuned to universal energies than most, and this influences my readings and my work. I have a passion for harmonics... the sacred resonant mathematical ratios of relationship, of proportion in design, of interval, as they manifest in music, voice, astrology, and sacred geometry. The same principles carry through with continuity.

From an astrological perspective, this major shift in intensification and acceleration has been increasing for years now. We are being called to let go of our old conditioning and habituation, to confront and transform the abuse of power, and to move beyond dualistic thinking and perceiving – the past ends now! The most important thing is to not fall into fear, because fear sucks the energy right out of you, and cuts you off from the light. When we are aligned with universal energy and flow, we are in our creativity and light, and the way forward is shown.

Did you know that astronomers are discovering new planets in our solar system? We have new 'dwarf planets' in Eris, Makemake, Haumea, and at the farthest reaches of the solar system, Sedna. Newly discovered planets indicate new aspects of consciousness coming into potentiality and awareness. It's time for us to make a major quantum leap in consciousness! We must move beyond our dissociation, our dualistic, competitive sense of self-entitlement, not to lose our individuality, but to move forward with it into realization that we are interdependent, all cells on this same Earth mother body, and to work responsibly in cooperation and compassion in Oneness consciousness.

The key is in harmonic solar/'soul-ar' soul-centered emergence and ascension, and for those who have done their work and are prepared to rise with it, it will be transformative, transcendent, healing, and full of beauty and wonder.

- Janis Page, M.A. is a professional astrologer, an award-winning composer, and a practitioner and teacher of cross-cultural sound healing. She teaches at Metropolitan State College of Denver. She holds a masters degree in Counseling and is a certified cross-cultural music healing practitioner (CCMHP). She lives in Denver, Colorado. www.RubyMala.com

"*The Sons and Daughters of God shall not walk in the New Garden with broken hearts and souls, this is a certainty.*" ~ Ascended Master Yeshua, through Argus El'iam

    From the time I was a small child, I knew that I was "different" and I always felt like I was out of place, and didn't belong here. Here, meaning on the Earth. When I was 4 years old as I sat playing with my toys up alone in my bedroom, a group of non-physical Light Beings or what some would call Angels appeared to me and basically laid out the origins and cosmology of the Universe and Earth to me, the Universal principles and mysteries of life and energy, and with that how Jesus (Yeshua) conducted his healing work. It was much like receiving a refresher course for what I already knew, lest I forget in time. They informed me that I would be going through what would appear as very difficult trials and tests in this lifetime and would "go dim" for a portion of my life, but it would all be for the greater good. The main piece they imparted to me, was not to forget who I *really* was and that there was a "grand plan" of which I was part and a greater reality always.

    At age twelve, when most boys my age were going through puberty and awakening to their sexual, individual selves, I went through my own *spiritual* awakening. I began a quest for the truth and what was *really* going on, my own cosmic behind the scenes investigation. I began to see the hypocrisy and distorted truth presented by many religions, including my own Catholic faith. I found I had two sets of eyes develop, the eyes in my head and what I call the *eyes of my heart*. The eyes of my heart were tuned into a very different reality than the former.

    Instead of focusing on my regular schoolwork, I had my head buried in parapsychology and metaphysical literature. As a new teen, rather than bumping my head against a buddy in a game of touch football, I was bumping my head against my bedroom ceiling during an experiment with astral projection. I would go outside at night and stare up at the starlit sky for hours and long to be back "home" where I belonged. I kept hearing the words, "mission, you are on a mission" in the back of my mind. I got the sense that I was part of some unseen group that I was selected to be on 'Earth' assignment.

It has been 50 years now since my Celestial Light Being friends had visited me and imparted their profound message to me, and I have been witnessing the amazing unfolding and perfection of all that has transpired since that time and my role in it all. I have come to see how people like myself have actually been trailblazers in the world, and how I have energetically forged a path, with others like myself, to make the way into this time easier for others to follow. Many of us have sensed the vibrational shifts on the planet for some time now. All souls incarnated into this earth experience at this particular juncture of time/space, are here to participate in this amazing shift. We are now metaphorically, if not literally standing at the gate of the New Garden and our hearts and souls are stirring and expanding with intense anticipation.

This shift represents a marker for the end of one grand cycle and the beginning of another. It is the convergence and alignment of universal cosmic energies that is part of a glorious evolutionary expansion of consciousness on all levels. The playing field we have been playing on is shifting dramatically. What this means in day to day life, is that what we see show up in our reality will be much more closely related to our thoughts, feelings, and intentions. In the time to come, we will play an important role in assisting many who are struggling to find deeper meaning and connection, and teach a way of being in the New Earth Garden; a way where heart and mind work together in a balanced harmonious way, and a way where seeing with the "eyes of the heart" will become more the norm than ever before.

- Argus El'iam is a multi-talented, transformational visionary artist, sonic (sound) healer, composer, writer, and workshop facilitator. He makes his home on the magical garden sanctuary of Kauai. www.ArgusEliam.com

~~~~~

"Love IS the Answer," (excerpt from ***The Emissary*** © 2010)

In his literary works Dr. Sigmund Freud proposed two states of being which he considered constant and universal: *Eros* (associated with a love for life and a tendency towards cohesion and unity) and the Death Drive (sometimes referred to as *Thatanos* with a mindset of destruction and forgetfulness). Eternally in opposition to each other, they force all living things in successive cycles to evolve or perish. But Freud would not allude to which one he thought would prevail in the end for humanity; then again, Freud was not responsible for Earth's creation.

Faced with the grim possibility of extinction, often living things will strive first for self preservation. This philosophy is not a new concept. You have probably seen evidence of it in fantasy films or real life events. However, it is also true that living creatures are often at their best when things are at their worst. In the final hour they have been observed to band together in innovative and compassionate ways – against insurmountable odds – to save every life where possible; the stuff of heroic tales with the good guys winning.

The unprecedented recent events have showcased a worldwide breakdown of economic, political, and religious status quos. The domino effect impacted every corner of the globe, jolting many out of a state of existence steeped in complacency and comfort. Faced with a more basic mode of survival, many are now awakening to what has been flowing through the ether in waves; an unspoken (the empathic way) consensus that either all work together on some level for the better good or all will perish. This paradigm shift in the living consciousness of the organism called Earth is beginning to take root and grow. It is not just humans experiencing these undercurrents it is also the flora, the fauna, and the mountains that are responding to the situation.

The possibility of what is coming is creating an organic desire for cohesion and unity. Instead of just a select few, every living thing is becoming open to participating in the process of conscious evolution. Despite what cataclysmic events may indicate, Divine Order for the preservation of Earth is at work here.

-- **Raline Starc**, Author and Artist

~~~~~~

The Shift means that healers, intuitives, aware, awake and otherwise-spiritualized souls need to "climb down the mountain" -- to use a timeless Buddhist metaphor -- in order to greet and guide the masses who are just starting out on their very first climb UP. Some of these folks will be in shock, some will feel lost or disoriented, and many will flounder. When energies build up without conscientious direction, or without maneuvering structures in place, damage too often occurs, both to oneself and to others. It is of utmost importance that Energy Medicine on all its levels be taken into the places that do not *know* to seek it out. Blue collar neighborhoods, third world shantytowns, prisons and inner city schools must be exposed to information which they direly need at this time. A person in unfortunate life circumstances, who feels an added energy "buzz" or opening, will likely choose to do something very unconstructive with it, if not downright destructive. Empaths, healers and seekers who have been on the journey for a while, or who caught the first waves of the shift, are perfectly poised to share their gifts, guidance or experience with those of meager exposure. Conscious minds *must* be willing to let go of comfort, to challenge themselves, and to perform seemingly heroic tasks. In face of the upcoming swell, it will take every Energy Shepherd available, to prevent stampedes all around the world."

- Sandra Mendes, M.F.A./A.P.P.
psychic dancer, writer, choreographer, somatic movement teacher and intuitive healer, writing from the bowels of Brazil.

~~~~~

The shift, from my perspective as an empath and Buddhist teacher, is a call to to dream our world into being. Jenkins and Calleman's text, the Mystery of 2012, references the Vedic Kali Yuga which parallels the Mayan calendar in indicating a time of complete transformation. Significantly, the text notes the Mayan prophecy does not come with a set of operating instructions. The outcome, what we do with this time that we have-- this is up to us.

It is my feeling that the heightened sensitivity and dreams so many of us, who are sensitive, have been experiencing are foreshadowings of possibility, a future which continues to shift and which through our collective energy work, and reinforcing of certain threads of possibility, can heal. In lucid dreams, I work consciously towards experiencing the threads of possible futures which reflect our highest visions: sustainable living practices, ecological communities.

In the Lotus Sutra, a Buddhist text which references the Kali Yuga, a teaching is brought forth which is core within Buddhism, related to the energy with which we meet these changing times: the Lion's Roar. The Lion's Roar is actually a great vow of compassion, which arises out of complete openness, transparency.

This teaching is shown in Ashokan (ancient Indian) art as four lions facing the four directions. If we move toward our life experience, not holding back anything, we have access to the highest energy, complete fearlessness. We find the courage to take off our armor, and our golden lion nature is revealed. Moment by moment this openness becomes a raw new place to live from, and our light moves others to awaken.

Through our practice of staying open, staying connected to our intentions of compassion, our practices of seeing how we are not separate from anything in the universe, we live our way into an enlightened world. One of the traits of sensitives is that we radiate our vibe to others, and they pick it up and learn from it.

Every action, every thought, is like a stone thrown into water, rippling in widening circles. And this is creating our world.

- Ji Hyang Padma is an intuitive astrologer and spiritual counselor who especially loves working with clients to help them access their own inner resources. She has taught workshops at The Omega Institute, Esalen Institute, Kripalu Institute and UCLA. She has trained intensively in Zen for nineteen years, including fifteen years as a nun in the Korean Zen tradition. She lives in Somerville, Massachusetts.
www.Natural-Wisdom.org

~~~~~

I have long been fascinated by beginnings and endings, boundaries and paradigm shifts. In the mind and heart of this natural born intuitive, it beckons with open arms, the opportunity to shift perception (the best definition I have heard of the word 'miracle'). It issues an invitation for people to step forward and take responsibility for the thoughts and literal energy we send out into the world. I do feel called to respond to that invitation, step up and raise a candle, along with others who have elected to say a heart-felt YES!

In my work with clients and students, I offer them the idea that there is always a choice in any given moment, between love and fear. We may remain trapped in fear's vicious grip or float in love's embrace. Far more than a "cosmic foo foo" concept or a throwback to my 1960's flower child existence, it is grounded in practical reality. It's as simple as observing what happens when in a room with people who are either delighted with their lives or who are simply going through the motions. It doesn't take intuitive abilities to sense the difference.

- Rev. Edie Weinstein, LSW is a work in progress. Her creative, career and spiritual paths have led her to become a writer, speaker, interfaith minister, reiki master, clown, greeting card text writer and social worker. She is the author of *The Bliss Mistress Guide To Transforming The Ordinary Into The Extraordinary.* www.LiveinJoy.com

~~~~~

A Channeling

The vessel of truth which each represents in potential, in potent emptiness, fragility and strength seeks the design of the creator with every breath. Let it be so. Let every breath recreate the divinity which is you, which is present in every cellular representation of the whole, the Universal imprint upon your being. Thusly created in inherent perfection, allow this potential to carve deeply into each place where light seemingly has not existed, into the depths of physical pain, the wells of loneliness, where cellular image holds memories of separation from the truth of Source Light presence. At one with it, the depth of disparity, of despair itself, becomes awakened to the truth that naught has been forgotten with the passage of time.

Each action represented by the holy form of the body has been recorded in truth within the record of time, and in recognition is illuminated by the Light of Truth. God is present. Light is Living, breathing through all and in your seeking, fills your vessel to encompass all that has felt lacking. The continual rebirth with every breath and release of impressions of the past represents a resolution and joyful release even in their remembrance as strife passing through your awareness. Glory be to God in the Highest, for it exists within each one of You. Forever whole, forever enlightened, let now the veils of camouflage be flung from your mind.

Your knowing is from the source fountain springing through every creation in existence. The truth of the coming times is that of focus on Joy. Focus on Light. In seeking the truth, it is a decision on What that Truth Will Be. It is your design. Make it holy and the manifestation of such certainly follows. Each strand, from which you are made, is a ribbon of God. And with that support continuing to unfurl in grace and beauty let your evolving awareness thusly grow. You do not relive the past yet with your choices.

Let the choice be Joy, Love in the Highest, and Peace will be so for all living representations of source Light. In the coming declarations of God seek not a scenario where all are not glowing in Realization of Oneness, for thusly that swings the Whole. Not in part does the Light of Joy wish to be represented reverberating and felt within the masses of Light Beings incarnated at this time. Let each question asked of you be answered with these words. Let each longing be soothed and the clarity of illuminated suffering diminish as the raising of light frequency manifests. You are present in perfection and moving through the waves of weighted time in perfection. Think not and worry not for the Forces of Light never cease to lift you upon their waves. In splendor the past unfurls like a grand song from the body as I Am re-birthed again and again through you. All is calm, all is bright.

- Margaret Gilfoyle is healer and channel who offers "Breath of Light" phone consultations and channelings with Beings of Light, spiritual masters, angels, and ascended healers. Margaret's work with the Breath of Light guidance began in 2003. She has since facilitated thousands of individual healing sessions, taught group classes and intensives, and received media coverage both in print and on radio. Her professional training includes Usui Reiki Master/Teacher through Reiki Master Zari Paristeh, traditional South American healing through Don Alberto Taxo, Elba Ortiz, Ipupiara and Cleicha and others, and Healing Touch through Healing Touch International.
www.OneHeartWorld.com

RESOURCE GUIDE

Check out the following websites for excellent information:

www.LDIntuitive.com
My friend Lawrence Porter offers remote healing, and has been gifted by the Divine with extraordinary abilities.
.

www.Sapaninka.com
Research and articles from Peru, including the plant medicine ayahuasca, devoted to building a New Spiritual Nation.

www.EmpathConnection.com
My empath and highly sensitive person resource center.

www.nderf.org
Near Death Experience Research Foundation offers thousands of reports, submitted by users, of individuals who have clinically died and crossed over to the other side.

"Mystical Hand"
by Argus El'iam

This art reflects how the hands can be focal points to express the Divine aspects of Creation within ourselves and also how they can operate as both receptors and transmitters of energy.

Argus El'iam is a multi-talented, transformational visionary artist, sonic (sound) healer, composer, writer, and workshop facilitator. He makes his home on the magical garden sanctuary of Kauai.

For more information on workshops and for ordering art prints, please visit: www.ArgusEliam.com

ABOUT THE AUTHOR

Dr. Michael R. Smith, Ph.D., N.C.C., has been a leader in the field of mind-body holistic healing for nearly 15 years. He is a past assistant editor of Counselor Education & Supervision Journal, one of the leading journals of the 50,000+ member American Counseling Association. He is the author of 8 research publications appearing in various scientific journals, and he has presented workshops in 20+ cities nationally.

In 2002, Michael received his Ph.D. in counseling from the University of Nevada-Reno, and that same year, Michael became Assistant Professor at the University of Wyoming, where he was a co-director of the masters degree counseling program. In 2003, Michael started an apprenticeship with several Native American shamans and healers. In a first-of-its-kind partnership, he secured $25,000 in grant funding to teach Native American healing methods to mainstream graduate counseling students.

In 2005, Michael made a decision to move out of the academic mainstream and relocated to Santa Fe, New Mexico. There he received a certification in Polarity therapy from the New Mexico Academy of Healing Arts and became a Registered Polarity Practitioner (R.P.P). He opened his own intuitive counseling and energy healing practice and he has continued to practice indigenous-based healing methods.

In March, 2008, Michael launched EmpathConnection.com, an online resource center for empaths and highly sensitive people, and he published his first book, *The Complete Empath Toolkit*. In 2009, Michael taught an empath workshop at the renowned Omega Institute in Rhinebeck, New York, and released two well-received CD audiobooks, *The Empath Experience*, and *Empath Intuition*.

In 2010, Michael announced the formation of an empath and highly sensitive person scholarship program. In 2012, he published *Awakening the Genesis Within* with LD Porter. He lives in the mountains of Evergreen, Colorado near Denver. In his spare time, he enjoys golf, his two cats, drumming, and a wonderfully joyful Yoga practice.

Printed in Great Britain
by Amazon.co.uk, Ltd.,
Marston Gate.